THE GERMANS IN AMERICA

by THEODORE

Albert Einstein . . . Ba
Charles Steinmetz—three men whose achievements
and interests are as diverse as the times in which
they lived. What common factor b...
together? Einstein, the celeb...
revealed ... the c...
again. Dr. Huebener
from G...
land. T...
in...

THE GERMANS IN AMERICA

THE GERMANS
IN AMERICA

THEODORE HUEBENER

CHILTON COMPANY · BOOK DIVISION
Publishers
PHILADELPHIA AND NEW YORK

Preface

In this book the author attempts to present, sympathetically and interestingly, the story of the Germans in America; that is, a short historical survey of their coming here and settling down, brief biographical sketches of eminent personalities among them, and a consideration of their contributions to the material and cultural development of the United States.

The German element is the largest ethnic group in our midst. It is estimated that about one-fifth of our population has German blood in its veins. As the following pages will show, Americans of German origin have participated in every major event in our history; they have deeply influenced a number of phases of our national life; and they have produced many noble characters.

On several occasions they have had to suffer severely—as other aliens have—because of their foreign origin. During the hysteria of war they were denounced as hyphenates. Although there were cultural isles here and there during the early part of the nineteenth century, the Germans have never formed an ethnic or a political bloc. They have become Americanized very rapidly, in many cases, losing their identity as Germans completely within one generation.

A careful examination of the record will show that no foreign group has surpassed the German-Americans in their devotion and loyalty to America.

T. H.

Acknowledgments

In preparing this brief volume, I have had to lean heavily on what still remains the authoritative work in this field, namely *The German Element in the United States* by Professor Albert B. Faust. Within its two volumes totaling 1321 pages, there is a vast amount of information which, however, takes the reader only to about 1925. In addition to sifting the material and approaching it from a different point of view, I have tried to bring the record up to date.

Another writer, whose works are indispensable in this field, especially with reference to more recent times, is Carl Wittke. For the subject of immigration, *We Who Built America: The Saga of the Immigrant* (New York, 1939), and for the story of German-American journalism, *The German-Language Press in America* are invaluable (University of Kentucky).

My information about the German Jews is taken largely from *Jews from Germany in the United States* by Eric E. Hirshler (Farrar, Straus & Cudahy, New York).

For valuable suggestions and comments I am grateful to Dr. Ludwig Oberndorf, Editor of the *Staats-Zeitung;* Professor Adolph Leschnitzer of City College; Dr. Jacob Greenberg, Associate Editor of Chilton; and my wife, Elizabeth.

T. H.

Contents

1 · The Early Colonial Period

1. A GERMAN DISCOVERS VINES IN VINELAND

The first German to put his foot on American soil was Tyrker, the foster father of Leif Ericson, the Norse leader whose ships reached the New World around the year A.D. 1000. The Norsemen sailed along the coast from Labrador down to New England, evidently planning a settlement somewhere.

According to the Norse saga, they discovered one evening that Tyrker was missing. Leif was much distressed and chose twelve men to accompany him in his search for the old man. They soon discovered him, quite gay and elated. In fact, he seemed to be hysterical with joy; he rolled his eyes, grinned, and spoke in his native German. Finally he addressed them in Norse, saying: "I have something new for you; I have found a grapevine." "Are you sure?" inquired Leif. "Certainly," replied Tyrker, "for I was born where there is no dearth of grapes." Thus, the land was called Wineland, or Vineland.

Five hundred years later, another German was responsible for the name given to the New World. In 1507, Martin Waldseemüller, born in Freiburg, Baden, and lecturing as a professor at the University of Dijon, published his *Cosmographiae Introductio* in which he describes the voyages of Vespucius and suggests the name "America" in honor of its discoverer, Americus Vespucius. The map accompanying the book was not discovered until about 1900. It was reproduced and published in London in 1903.

Although the Germans did not engage in voyages of discovery and exploration like the Spaniards, the Portuguese, the

1

French, the Dutch, and the English, they appeared in various parts of North and South America in the very earliest times. It is thought that there were some Alsatians and Hessians among the company of French Protestants (Huguenots) who settled at Port Royal, South Carolina, in 1562. Four years later, the Spaniard, Menendez, destroyed the settlement.

2. THE "DAMNED DUTCH"

According to the account of Captain John Smith, there were also Germans in the colony at Jamestown in 1607. Considerable rivalry and irritation developed between them and the English "gentlemen," for they were the artisans of the colony. Despite their usefulness, Captain Smith had difficulties with them and referred to them as the "damned Dutch."

The confusion of "Dutch" and "German" arose among the English-speaking population from the fact that the Germans called themselves "Deutsch." In fact, the Netherlands was part of the Holy Roman (German) Empire until the Treaty of Westphalia in 1648, and the Germans of the Lower Rhine and the Dutch were, therefore, similar in background.

From Smith's account, it appears that the "Dutchmen" preferred the kindly Indians who supplied them with food, to the bickering English who treated them with disdain. Smith himself notes that the Poles and the Dutchmen had to make pitch, tar, glass, and soap, while many of the English were idlers. In his *True Travels* he says: "Adventurers never did know what a day's work was, except the Dutchmen and Poles and some dozen others. For all the rest were poor gentlemen, tradesmen, serving-men, libertines, and such like, ten times more fit to spoil a commonwealth, than either to begin one or to help to maintain one."

Germans continued to come to Virginia, despite the failure of Jamestown. As early as 1608, German glass blowers appeared, and in 1620 four millwrights from Hamburg came to Virginia to erect the first sawmills. Germans also set up a tobacco plantation in Cavalier County, and in 1653, vintners came from Heidelberg and introduced German wines to the

2

New World. Because of the growth of the German settlement, the county records of Richmond appear partially written in German script.

3. MINUIT BUYS MANHATTAN

The largest number of Germans, however, were in New Netherlands which was then the Hudson Valley from Manhattan as far north as Albany. It is estimated that from one-fourth to one-third of the entire population came from Germany.

The first director general of New Amsterdam was Peter Minuit (Minnewit), born in Wesel on the Rhine. He arrived in the colony in May, 1626, with almost absolute ruling powers. His predecessors had not been successful, but the determined Minuit rapidly transformed the colony into a well-organized and prosperous community. He bought the island of Manhattan, some 22,000 acres, from the Indians for sixty Dutch guilders, or about twenty-four dollars in gold. At the Battery he erected Fort Amsterdam, built of heavy stone. The Indians did not dare to attack, and New Amsterdam soon became a thriving town. Cattle and horses were supplied by the Dutch West India Company, good crops were raised, and a profitable fur trade with the Indians sprang up. By 1631, the exportation of furs amounted to 130,000 guilders. Under Minuit's direction, the shipbuilding industry flourished, producing a vessel of eight hundred tons, a large ship for those times.

Without Minuit's approval, the Dutch West India Company established the patroon system which hindered the development of the colony. Each of the patroons became a manor lord with semi-feudal privileges over a large tract of land. Dissension arose, and Minuit was recalled. When he left in 1632, New Netherlands was in excellent economic condition. Since Minuit was not exonerated in Holland, he offered his services to the King of Sweden. The Swedes were interested in establishing a colony in the New World and listened eagerly to his proposals. At the end of 1637, Minuit returned to

3

America with a warship and a transport carrying fifty immigrants. He arrived in Delaware Bay in April, 1638. With eminent skill he prevented the English and the Dutch from interfering with his plans for colonization. Near the present site of Wilmington, Delaware, he built Fort Christina, so named in honor of the Swedish Queen.

His experience in building up New Amsterdam now stood him in good stead. As a result, that first year the profitable fur trade in Fort Christina amounted to thirty thousand guilders. New settlers came from Holland and Germany, and the Swedish West India Company did very well. His colony barely three years old, Minuit died in 1641 and lies buried at Fort Christina.

The Germans, rather than the Swedes, played a leading role in developing New Sweden. Hendrick Huygen from Cleve on the Rhine, Minuit's brother-in-law, was the commissary. From 1640 to 1643, another German, Peter Hollender Ridder, headed the colony. He was followed by Johann Printz, a German nobleman whose real name was Prinz Edler von Buchen. He had brought with him fifty-four German families from Pomerania. The last head of the colony was Heinrich von Elswich, a merchant from Luebeck. Consequently, German became the diplomatic language used between New Sweden and New Amsterdam.

However, in 1655, New Sweden became part of New Netherlands under the administration of the irascible Peter Stuyvesant.

Peter Stuyvesant, who had been governor of Curaçao and had lost a leg in battle, came to New Amsterdam in 1647. He was an energetic but frequently tactless individual who easily became enraged. Despite the complaints about his rule, the thriving community continued to grow.

In the beginning the colony was rather cosmopolitan. A Jesuit priest, who visited New Amsterdam in 1643, recorded eighteen spoken languages in the settlement with a population that included Germans, French, Swedes, Spaniards, Italians, Turks, and Jews. However, the character of the colony changed as a constant stream of English settlers arrived, gradually settling Long Island. English was being spoken more and more, and this proved to be a vital factor in New Amsterdam's future. Wedged in between New England and the other English colonies, the colony occupied a crucial position geographically. It divided the British possessions both commercially and politically. Charles II solved the problem quite simply. He said to his brother, the Duke of York: "I shall give you New Netherlands, but you will have to take it." "But we are at peace. What will the Dutch think?" asked the Duke. "Do not worry about that; it is really our land, it belongs to us."

So a fleet was sent across the ocean. It entered the harbor of New Amsterdam on September 6, 1664. Stuyvesant was prepared to fight. When Colonel Nicholls, the English commander, sent him a conciliatory letter, the fiery Dutchman tore it up and threw the pieces on the floor. A bystander picked them up, pasted them together, and read the message to a group of citizens. The terms of the British were accepted; they were invited to come in; and thus New Amsterdam became New York. An angry, defeated Stuyvesant retired to his farm, which was on the present site of Union Square, and there he died.

4. JACOB LEISLER, MARTYR TO FREEDOM

The second governor of New York was a German, Jacob Leisler. Born in Frankfurt, he had come to New Amsterdam in 1660 as a soldier in the service of the Dutch West India Company. By trading skillfully with the Indians, he became wealthy; through marriage, he entered the Dutch aristocracy. Only three vessels were owned in New York, and one of them belonged to him. When he was captured by pirates of Tunis in 1678, a ransom of five hundred pounds was paid for him.

Leisler was a man of unusual intelligence, courage, and generosity. When a group of Huguenots landed in New York in 1689, he bought them a large tract of land on the site of the present city of New Rochelle. He also saved several Hugue-

5

not families from years of servitude by paying the sums they owed as redemptioners for their passage money.

The Dutch were dissatisfied with British rule, particularly because James II had combined the colonies of New England, New York, and New Jersey under one governor, Edmund Andros. While Governor Andros was in England, Francis Nicholson acted as lieutenant governor. News arrived that William of Orange had landed in England, and there was much excitement among the Dutch population, who naturally looked to the public-spirited and energetic Leisler as a leader. At that point, Nicholson made the rash remark, "I would rather see the city on fire than take the impudence of such fellows as you," to a disobedient officer. Word spread that the governor was about to set the city on fire. A mob gathered, formed a small army, and marched to Leisler's house. Leisler refused to assume leadership, but Lieutenant Stoll led the mob to the fort. Nicholson was captured without offering any resistance. Later on he fled.

On June 8, 1689, a committee of citizens appointed Leisler commander-in-chief of the city, until the arrival of a new governor from England. News soon arrived of the coronation of William and Mary, and Leisler made preparations for an appropriate ceremony. The magistrate and the aldermen, who had refused to join, were dismissed. The Committee of Safety appointed Leisler supreme commander of the Colony in August, 1689.

Leisler prepared a careful report of everything that had happened and dispatched Lieutenant Stoll to England with it. Neither Stoll nor the report was favorably received by the King, for Nicholson had prejudiced the King against Leisler and his representative, Stoll. William of England declared that the popular party, which Leisler led, was hostile to the established Church as well as disloyal to the new King himself. Meanwhile, the aristocrats in the Colony denounced him as a demagogue and a Jacobite.

Albany refused to recognize the government of Leisler. Thereupon, the new governor sent a company of militia under the command of his son-in-law, Jacob Milborne, to seize the fort at Albany. However, the force was too weak to carry out this order and had to withdraw. The fugitive aristocrats sent complaints to London, accusing Leisler of rebellion against the King.

At the beginning of December, 1689, a royal messenger arrived with a letter addressed to Francis Nicholson or those who were administering the laws in the "Province of New York." The messenger was brought to New York and handed the letter to Leisler, who, on December 11, 1689, assumed the title of lieutenant governor.

His enemies, however, had not given up. After an unsuccessful attempt to capture him on the street one day, the ringleaders were seized, thrown into prison, and charged with high treason. After being sentenced to death, the two men, Bayard and Nicolls, pleaded for mercy, and Governor Leisler magnanimously relented.

Leisler had been lieutenant-governor for only a month when the French attacked New York. In January, 1690, the fort at Schenectady was taken, burned, and plundered. Albany was saved by Leisler's quick action in sending troops to its defense.

The lieutenant-governor realized that the French were a formidable foe and that united action was necessary. Hence, in April, 1690, he invited the governors of Massachusetts, New Jersey, Pennsylvania, Maryland, and Virginia to meet in New York. This historic conference, held in May of 1690, was the first American congress, and it was followed by a number of others that finally resulted in the Continental Congress.

The six governors decided to equip both an army to conquer Canada and to send a fleet to take Quebec, but dissension and misunderstanding wrecked the plans for the land expedition. Stormy winds doomed the attack by sea to failure. Despite Leisler's courageous and intelligent action, his efforts were not crowned with success. Huge debts were incurred; taxes were imposed and Leisler's enemies became increasingly truculent. At the end of the year a new governor, Colonel Henry Sloughter, was appointed by the crown.

During a storm at sea the ships became separated and Major Ingoldsby, the second in command, arrived in New York. Leisler refused to yield his office until Colonel Sloughter arrived. Some bitter fighting occurred, and Leisler was confined to one of the forts. On March 19, 1691, Sloughter arrived. He freed Bayard and Nicolls from prison and incarcerated Leisler and eight of his friends.

Charged with rebellion, illegal taxation, and treason, Leisler was condemned to death by his personal enemies who sat as judges. They filled Sloughter with wine in order to secure his signature on the death warrant for Leisler and his son-in-law, Milborne. On a cold, wet May 16, both men were hanged at a scaffold erected at Pearl and Centre Streets, the site of the Tombs prison.

It was soon evident that the execution of Leisler had been a grave miscarriage of justice. His son began proceedings in the British courts, and after years of litigation, Parliament finally reversed the charges against Leisler and Milborne in 1695, exonerated both completely, and restored the property that had been confiscated. Three years later, their bodies were removed from under the gallows and interred in the cemetery of the Dutch Church in Exchange Place. Over fifteen hundred persons took part in the ceremonies, and the event attracted attention all over the Colonies. Increase Mather, one of the prominent figures in colonial politics, declared that Leisler had been "barbarously murdered."

Leisler was the first great representative of popular government in the Colonies. His calling of the first congress was a most memorable act. His integrity and zeal were transmitted to a number of his descendants, one of whom was Governor Morris.

2 ⋅ Pennsylvania: "The Holy Experiment"

1. PENN AND PASTORIUS

The first Germans to found a permanent settlement in America were a group of religious refugees chiefly from the Palatinate. They came to Germantown, Pennsylvania (now a part of Philadelphia), in 1683.

It was William Penn who was largely instrumental in bringing them to America. Inspired with missionary zeal, the young Englishman visited Holland and Germany in 1671 and 1677 to gain adherents for the faith of the Quakers. As early as 1655, George Fox, the founder of the Society of Friends, had sent messengers to the Continent. When Penn arrived, he found a small community of Quakers near Worms in a village called Kriegsheim which, strangely enough, means "home of war."

The Rhineland was at this time fertile ground for a spread of the Quaker teachings, inasmuch as there were numerous small, pietistic sects that held similar ideas. They stressed the inward life, spirituality as opposed to dogma, simplicity and purity of living, and opposition to war and violence. In addition to the Quakers, there were the Mennonites, the Schwenkfelders, the Dunkards, and the Pietists. Since by law only the Catholic, the Lutheran, and the Reformed churches were tolerated, these sects were considered illegal.

William Penn—who is said to have preached in German—received a warm and cordial reception when he spoke along the Rhine and in Frankfurt. Although he made some converts to Quakerism, Penn's great achievement was not religious,

9

but rather political and social. It was his appearance on the Rhine that started the waves of emigration from southwest Germany and caused hundreds of thousands of Germans to seek a new home in America.

In lieu of the payment of sixteen thousand pounds in sterling, which the British government owed Admiral Penn, his son, William, was given a tract of land known as Pennsylvania. Shortly after the issuing of the royal charter, a brief description of the province was published. Among other things, it pointed out the advantages for immigrants. This book, which was translated into German, came to the attention of Pietists in Frankfurt. They were intrigued by the possibilities of life in the New World and formed a company for the purpose of immigration. Through Benjamin Furley, Penn's agent, they purchased fifteen thousand acres of land in the wilderness. Later, the Frankfurt Company, as it was called, extended its holdings to twenty-five thousand acres, offering a share of five thousand acres for one hundred pounds. Although there was much enthusiasm about life in the New World, none of the Frankfurt circle—who apparently were cultured and well-to-do individuals—came to America.

Only their agent, Francis Daniel Pastorius, did. He was a well-educated and widely traveled young lawyer who became so deeply interested in the project that he decided to cast in his lot with the emigrants. He sailed from Deal, England, in June of 1683, on the ship *America* with a number of men and women of humble origin. While crossing the ocean, Pastorius won the friendship of a Welsh physician, Thomas Lloyd, an Oxford scholar, who later became the president of the Provincial Council. Since Pastorius knew no English at that time and Lloyd was ignorant of German, they conversed in Latin. Penn was delighted with Pastorius, who landed on August 20, and gave him a cordial reception. Twice a week the young lawyer dined at the governor's house.

The cultured Pastorius was amused by the poorly built houses of the city of Philadelphia which had been laid out only two years before and which consisted, as he records in his diary, largely of woods and brushwood. He writes, "A striking impression this made upon me, coming from London, Paris, Amsterdam, and Ghent."

The first company of actual immigrants from Krefeld set out six weeks later on the vessel *Concord* commanded by Captain Jeffreys. The devout company of Quakers and Mennonites consisted of thirteen heads of families. The fare was five pounds—half fare for children under twelve. The journey was a smooth one and on October 6, 1683, the vessel arrived safely in Philadelphia. This date is the one that is accepted by German-Americans as the beginning of their history in the United States.

Pastorius had made the arrangements for their departure from Kriegsheim and Krefeld, and he also provided for them when they arrived in Philadelphia. The Frankfurt Company had bought twenty-five thousand acres of land, and the Krefelders, eighteen thousand. The new arrivals founded a settlement six miles above the city which they named "Deutschstadt." Since this was difficult to pronounce, the name was soon changed to Germantown which is now in Philadelphia.

In his diary, *Grund und Lagerbuch,* Pastorius describes the severe hardships of the early settlers, but lauds their "Christian endurance and indefatigable industry." Pastorius shared their difficulties and lived in a wooden shack, fifteen feet by thirty, with oil-soaked paper for windows. Despite this, he maintained his humor and his scholarship throughout. Governor Penn laughed heartily when he read the motto the young lawyer had put over the wretched dwelling: *Parva domus sed amica bonis, procul este profani.* (Small is my house, it welcomes the good man; let the godless one stay away.)

The industries that the settlers had brought from Krefeld stood them in good stead. There were skillful weavers among them who produced so much that a store was opened in Philadelphia. They laid out vineyards and raised flax. Within a short time a wide variety of tradesmen, including carpenters, locksmiths, shoemakers, and tailors, appeared in the area. Several of the local products, especially the textiles, soon se-

11

cured an excellent reputation for the inhabitants of German-town. The first paper mill in the Colonies was established in Germantown by William Ruttinghausen (Rittenhouse) in 1690.

Germantown grew rapidly and soon incorporated smaller neighboring communities like Crefeld and Kresheim, all along the same road. In Germantown, which was closest to Phila-delphia, the road was sixty-feet-wide and lined with peach trees. The modest but comfortable dwellings each stood on three acres of land devoted to trees, flowers, and vegetables. A cross street forty feet in width led to the market place. It was a thriving community of tradesmen, farmers, and gardners. Pastorius admired the activity about him and deplored the vanity of book learning, remarking, "never have metaphysics and Aristotelian logic made of a savage a Christian, far less earned a loaf of bread."

Six years after its founding in 1689, Germantown was incor-porated as a town, and Pastorius had the honor of being the first mayor, an office he held four different times. It was an extremely peaceful and law-abiding community. Crime was practically nonexistent. The court sat every six weeks but fre-quently adjourned because there was no business. Occasionally a fine was levied for neglect of fences or a rare case of drunken-ness. Two amusing incidents were recorded: a certain Müller was locked up because of trying to smoke a hundred pipes of tobacco in one day as the result of a wager; and Caspar Karsten was put in the jug for calling the policeman a rogue.

However, hardly a case of drunkenness appears, although beer was brewed, and there was a saloon. Evidently the city fathers were anxious to prevent any possibility of intoxication, for during a half-day the sturdy burgher might purchase only a quarter of a pint of rum or a quart of beer. No wonder there were no drunks!

A peculiar situation, however, which has been characteristic of German communities up to the present, is the apathy dis-played toward politics and public affairs. It was difficult to get citizens to serve in public office. In fact, the situation became so critical that those who declined to serve were fined three pounds.

Pastorius was much annoyed by this lack of interest in public affairs, and he complained to William Penn about it. He himself set an excellent example in his unselfish and untiring devotion to the community. In fact, the progress and prosperity of Germantown were due largely to his leadership. He served as burgomaster, town clerk, notary, and member of the Provincial Council. He despised personal gain and asked for only small fees. He was the head of the Quaker School in Philadelphia from 1698 to 1700, and, in 1702, he took charge of the school in Germantown which included a night school for adults.

This must have been highly gratifying to Pastorius, for he was primarily a scholar. In his youth he had studied at the Universities of Altdorf, Strassburg, Basel, and Jena. His learning was encyclopedic, and he had mastered a number of languages. His *Bee Hive* is a neatly written collection of historical, literary, geographical, and poetical material in English, Latin, German, French, Dutch, and Italian.

Pastorius, however, was not only a diligent scholar and a conscientious public officer; he was also a courageous idealist. Under his leadership, a group of Germans met on April 18, 1688, and made the first formal protest against Negro slavery —over 150 years before the Civil War. The document, in the handwriting of Pastorius, was sent to the meeting of the Quakers who gracefully avoided the issue.

2. SECTARIANS GALORE

Because of the homogeneity of its inhabitants, Germantown remained a German city, at least during the eighteenth century. In fact, it was the social and cultural center for the Germans of the Middle Atlantic area. Immigrants went out from here to settle in the other counties of Pennsylvania and in the Midwest. Books and newspapers were published in German. The fairs and industrial activity attracted people from other communities. Wealthy citizens of Philadelphia began to build summer residences there. As time went on, Germantown lost its German character.

The original settlers had come because of deep religious convictions which continued to live for a long time because of the arrival of a number of mystics. Their leader, Johann Jakob Zimmermann, died in Rotterdam on the eve of his embarkation for America in 1693. Nevertheless, his ideas regarding the imminent end of the world were brought to Germantown by Johann Kelpius. He and his followers founded a sort of monastic order on the banks of the Wissahickon Creek, and his successors started the Ephrata Community in Lancaster County.

In addition to a number of individual religious leaders— who often disagreed violently—there were many pietistic sects that were drawn to Pennsylvania. After the first arrivals in Germantown, the next group of immigrants consisted of Swiss Mennonites who came about 1710. They settled on ten thousand acres in what is now Lancaster County. Like the Quakers, they believed in separation of church and state, freedom of conscience, simplicity of dress, and refused to take oaths or bear arms. They were diligent and thrifty and made Lancaster County a garden spot.

About nine years after the Mennonites, came the so-called Dunkards—*Tunker* in German, from *eintunken,* "to immerse." They also shared the doctrines of the Quakers and the Mennonites. They founded settlements in Berks County and Conestoga where the outstanding figure among the Dunkards was Christopher Sauer, who published a widely read German newspaper. From his press came the German Bible—the first book published in a European language in America.

Despite the meekness and kindliness of these small sects, religious differences continually arose. One of the Dunkards, a Conrad Beissel, organized a society of Seventh Day Baptists and founded the Cloister of Ephrata in Cocalico. He, too, owned a press, and the mystical writings he printed are still extant.

These smaller groups were outnumbered by the Lutherans,

14

the German Reformed and the United Brethren. The Lutherans had a very energetic leader in the person of Heinrich Melchior Mühlenberg who had studied in Göttingen. Under his ministry, the famous Zion Church was built. Consecrated in 1769, it was for many years the largest church in Philadelphia. Because of its size, it was frequently used for important public gatherings. It was there on December 26, 1799, at the funeral services of George Washington, that Henry Lee pronounced the memorable words, "First in war, first in peace, first in the hearts of his countrymen."

Mühlenberg, who ruled the Lutheran church with a firm hand, was on friendly terms with the Episcopalian and the German Reformed churches. The latter, who followed the doctrines of Calvin and Zwingli, had a capable leader in Michael Schlatter, who had been sent to the Colonies in 1746 by the Dutch Reformed Synod. Despite his success as an organizer, he had difficulties which forced him to give up his pulpit in Philadelphia and become a Revolutionary War chaplain and a chaplain in the Royal American Regiment, composed mainly of Germans.

The relations between Mühlenberg and Schlatter were cordial, for both men were of the same character. Although they belonged to different churches, their religious and political views were quite similar. Vigorous fighters, they counteracted the nonresistant attitude of the Quakers, the Mennonites, the Moravians, and other sectarians. In fact, they urged armed resistance to the British.

Although the pietistic groups refused to engage in armed struggle, they made notable contributions to the cultural and spiritual life of Pennsylvania. This was particularly true of the Moravians or United Brethren. In German they were called *Herrnhutter,* after Herrnhut, the estate in Saxony to which Count von Zinzendorf had invited them. In fact, it was Count von Zinzendorf who named the settlement on the Lehigh River Bethlehem.

The count was courageous and farsighted. His two great ideals were the conversion of the Indians and the union of the various Protestant sects. The latter proved a failure; the former, a success. The Moravians are credited with being the most effective Indian missionaries in American history.

3. JOURNALISM FLOURISHES

There were several printers in the Colony of Pennsylvania, and the number of German books, almanacs, and tracts published by them is amazing. Some of these were in Pennsylvania Dutch, the oldest immigrant language still in use in the United States. It is a mixture of South German and English, but it has attained a vigor and a flexibility which make it an adequate vehicle for poetry as well as prose.

Among the smaller sects, the Dunkards were the first to make use of the printing press. Christopher Sauer, one of their number, published a German edition of *Pilgrim's Progress* in the year 1754. By 1754, over two hundred different publications were issued from the various German presses in the Colonies, the great majority of them from Pennsylvania.

Although Benjamin Franklin made some disparaging remarks about the stupidity of the Pennsylvania Germans, he began the first German newspaper, the *Philadelphische Zeitung*. The editor was a French "language master" whose German was not too sound. The first issue of the paper appeared May 6, 1732; it expired after the second issue.

Success, however, greeted the efforts of Christopher Sauer who had come to America in 1724. Although trained as a tailor, he was a farmer by trade; he also made button molds, cast stoves, dealt in herbs, repaired clocks, made ink, and sold Franklin stoves. Having built his own press, he began printing books in 1738.

On August 20, 1739, he issued his newspaper, *Der Hoch Deutsche Pennsylvanische Geschichtsschreiber*. A few years later, Sauer opened his own paper mill and made his own types. His paper, the name of which was changed to *Germantauner Zeitung*, appeared quite regularly and was successfully continued by his son upon Sauer's death.

A number of other papers and magazines made their appearance in German. The only publisher, however, who could challenge the Sauers, was Henry Miller, editor of *Der Wöchentliche Philadelphische Staatsbote*, founded in 1762. Miller, who was born in Waldeck, had come to America with Count von Zinzendorf, the leader of the Moravians. He was employed by Benjamin Franklin and printed books in German and English. Miller's paper circulated not only in Pennsylvania, but also in New York, Maryland, and Virginia. A feud arose between him and the Sauers, for the latter were loyalists, and Miller supported the Revolution. In fact, he claimed the proud distinction of having been the first to publish the adoption of the Declaration of Independence. He printed the entire document in German type on July 5, 1776.

Sauer and Miller were the leading newspaper publishers. There were five successful German papers before the Revolution; by 1808, there were fourteen. Between 1732 and the end of the century, no fewer than thirty-eight German papers had appeared in Pennsylvania.

4. THE GERMAN SCHOOLMASTER
IN THE COLONIES

It is interesting to note the intellectual exchange between Germany and New England in the earliest times. This consisted of the correspondence of Cotton Mather and August Hermann Francke, the head of the pietistic wing of the Lutheran Church at Halle where he had founded a large orphan asylum. Francke had achieved international fame with his institutions, and a number of colleges and orphanages in the Colonies were modeled on them.

The correspondence between Mather and Francke was astoundingly heavy for an age without airmail and parcel post. The Boston theologian in 1709 sent a collection of 160 books and tracts on pietism to Halle, together with cash contributions for Francke's philanthropies. The German theologian was equally expansive: he replied with a letter of sixty-nine pages, written in Latin, in which he described his various institutions. Cotton Mather was much impressed. He

17

printed an account in Latin of Francke's enterprises and made plans for the establishment of similar institutions in Massachusetts.

The correspondence went on for another generation, for the sons of the two theologians continued the exchange which was concerned primarily with the organization of educational institutions. In those days schools were almost entirely within the domain of the churches, and the teachers were commonly ministers. Thus, the two professions were almost synonymous. When no pastor could be secured for a smaller community, the teacher usually read the Scriptures and delivered the sermons.

Some of these German teachers were men of considerable learning. The most distinguished among them was Francis Daniel Pastorius, the founder of Germantown and the friend of William Penn. He was the first German teacher in America. He served in the English Quaker School in Philadelphia from 1698 to 1700 and took charge of the first German school which was established in Germantown in 1702.

For a beginning educational enterprise in a colonial settlement, this school possessed a number of remarkable features. It was coeducational, and it maintained a night school for adults and for those who were employed. It was supported not only by the fees paid by the pupils, but also by voluntary contributions.

The basis of education in the Colonies was the ability to read and write and cipher—in other words, the three R's. It was also considered important to be well-grounded in the Bible and to write a clear, legible hand. In the church schools German was the language of instruction, and English was frequently not taught at all.

On the other hand, there were a number of enlightened teachers who introduced some startlingly modern practices. As an example, one may cite Christopher Dock, who taught in a school founded by the Mennonites as early as 1706. Dock was active for more than half a century (1714–71) and was a leader in his profession. He substituted the law of love for the

18

birch rod and was the first to use the blackboard. In 1750, he wrote what is undoubtedly the first pedagogical work published in America, *Schulordnung*. It was printed by Christopher Sauer of Philadelphia. In his book Dock displayed nobility of character and a keen insight into child psychology. He stressed the development of character as well as the training of the mind, and he placed morality and conduct before scholarship.

The other sectarians, such as the Schwenkfelders and the Moravians, also set up schools. The Moravians established not only schools at Nazareth, Bethlehem, and Lititz, but also academies for young women. These became very popular and were patronized by the non-German population as well as by Moravians. Their seminary in Bethlehem, founded in 1749, is the oldest school of its type in America.

The schools of the Lutheran and the Reformed church were the most numerous, since these were the two dominant religious groups in the German settlements. Mühlenberg, the leader of the Lutherans, and Schlatter, the head of the Reformed, paid much attention to their schools. Christopher Sauer, the printer and publisher, also took a deep interest in the German schools, particularly the Germantown Academy, founded in 1761.

Benjamin Franklin, that alert mind and universal genius, became interested in the education of the Germans with special reference to their mastery of English. One might say that he laid the foundations for what has become practically a permanant part of the American curriculum, a course in English for foreigners.

Franklin, however, was no narrow-minded nativist. Indeed, he believed strongly in a knowledge of foreign languages. In planning the curriculum for the Public Academy of the City of Philadelphia, which later developed into the University of Pennsylvania, he recommended the study of French and German besides English. The Academy grew into a college. In 1754, the trustees appointed William Creamer (Krämer) Professor of the French and German languages. He held this position until his retirement in 1775. Franklin, incidentally, was the first American to visit a German university. While in Göttingen, Hanover, in 1766, he stopped at the University where the Royal Society of Science honored him by making him a member.

Franklin's visit to Göttingen made a deep impression on Benjamin Smith Barton, a young resident of Lancaster. After studying natural science and medicine in Edinburgh and London, he went to the University of Göttingen where he received the degree of M.D. in 1789. He was the first American to become a Göttingen doctor.

Franklin recommended the teaching of modern languages in the Philadelphia Academy. The ancient languages, however, were not to be neglected. Through the influence of several clergymen on the Board of Trustees, Latin and Greek were introduced, Johann Christoph Kunze, a minister and a teacher of the classics, was appointed to teach the ancient tongues through the medium of German.

In 1787, the Assembly of Pennsylvania incorporated a German college in the county of Lancaster "for the instruction of youth in German, English, Latin, Greek, and other learned languages, in theology, and in the useful arts, sciences, literature." In honor of the largest contributor and earnest advocate of its founding it was named Franklin College.

Despite these auspicious beginnings and excellent schools, German influence on American education was not lasting. English and French influences penetrated more deeply. It was not until the latter half of the nineteenth century—and then through American educators rather than German-Americans—that German educational ideas and practices made a deep impression on American education.

3 · Germans in All the Colonies

1. THE PALATINES

During the sixteenth century, a large proportion of the inhabitants of the Palatinate (Pfalz) on the Rhine joined the Reformed church. During the Thirty Years War (1618–48), the Palatinate was repeatedly devastated by the contending armies. The pathetic Frederick V, the Winter King, took over the leadership of the Protestant cause, but was badly defeated in Bohemia. General Tilly, the Catholic commander, carried the war into his own country and laid it waste. The ruined land did not fare much better when its supposed friends, the Swedes under Gustavus Adolphus, came along. The final blow came with the Spaniards under Gallas, who exceeded all their predecessors in cruelty and brutality.

The next invaders were the French and the Bavarians in 1639. Their depredations in 1644 were so thorough that they left the land practically a desert. The successor of the Winter King, the Elector Karl Ludwig, was just beginning to make some progress in restoring the land to prosperity when it was invaded by the troops of Louis XIV. The beautiful castle of Heidelberg and the city of Mannheim were burned during the winter of 1688–89. The greed and the cruelty of the invaders reduced the population to complete poverty.

Although Karl Ludwig had been a Catholic, he had treated the Protestants with tolerance. But his fanatical successors ruled the land with an iron hand and mercilessly persecuted the Lutherans and the Reformed. It was no wonder, then, that the impoverished and wretched population should look to emigration as their only salvation. Their thoughts were turned toward America through the words of William Penn and through what seemed like an invitation from Queen Anne of England to settle in her transatlantic colonies. This was due to the bond of a common Protestant faith and to the fact that the royal families were related. Elizabeth, the daughter of James I, had married Frederick V, the Elector of the Palatinate, and had lived with him in Heidelberg Castle.

Through the War of the Spanish Succession in 1707, a section of the Palatinate on the left of the Rhine was devastated, and thousands were rendered homeless. A more energetic native, Joshua von Kocherthal, applied to an English agency in Frankfurt for permission to take sixty persons with him to England. Since they were without means of support when they reached London, the generous Queen provided for them. Kocherthal asked whether they could not go to the Colonies, whereupon the Lords of Trade decided to send them to New York. On the same ship with Lord Lovelace, the new governor, they set forth after having been naturalized as British subjects. They were chiefly carpenters, smiths, and weavers.

They arrived in New York in October of 1708 and were delighted with the beauty of the Hudson River which reminded them of the Rhine. Lord Lovelace gave them a tract of land, apportioning fifty acres to every individual. A settlement was founded which they named Neuburg (now Newburgh).

In 1709, Lord Lovelace, who had helped and befriended them, died. The Palatines, as they were known, had to appeal to the colonial government for assistance. This was granted to them. Since the soil around Newburgh was not particularly fertile, they sold their holdings to Dutch and English newcomers and moved north to Schoharie or south to Pennsylvania.

Kocherthal, who served as farmer, minister, and community leader, went to England in 1710 and returned to New York with another company of Palatines. Although he organized a Lutheran Church in West Camp, he was deeply respected by the Reformed. The provincial authorities also valued his judgment and frequently consulted him on temporal matters.

The success of Kocherthal in securing the help of the British Queen encouraged many others to look to the New World. Large numbers of Palatines migrated to England because of religious persecution, political oppression, and economic ruin. Most of them went by way of Rotterdam. The migratory movement began in May of 1709; by October, there were thirteen thousand Palatines in London. Although the city was large and prosperous, it was not prepared for such a large influx of foreigners. The authorities and private individuals, however, displayed unusual generosity and provided the Palatines with food and shelter for some months.

The religious issue always played a dominant role. Since this was primarily an enterprise for assistance to Protestants, Christian charity was not extended to the Catholics, who constituted about one-tenth of the Palatines. They were either converted or sent back in wretched condition. Visiting London at the time were several Indian chiefs. At the sight of these pathetic immigrants, the Indians generously offered them a free tract of land on the Schoharie in New York, a gesture which should have filled the bigots with shame.

When the Palatines were ready to be moved, a first contingent of five hundred families was sent to the province of Munster in Ireland where they settled down. The second group, which consisted of more than six hundred families, was shipped in 1709 to the Carolinas. Under the leadership of Graffenried and Michell, two natives of Bern, Switzerland, they founded the settlement of Newbern at the mouth of the Neuse River in North Carolina. The largest contingent, some three thousand persons, under the leadership of Colonel Robert Hunter, the new governor of the Colony, sailed in 1710 for New York.

The accommodations were so wretched that 773 passengers died of fever; also one of the ships was lost off the east end of Long Island, an incident which was immortalized by Whittier. Nevertheless, a good many survived the trip, and New York found itself unprepared for such a large number of newcomers. Because of the many deaths, there were children who had lost their parents. These orphans were taken by the authorities and apprenticed to tradesmen. Among the forty-one boys was John Peter Zenger, who later made history by his courageous fight for freedom of the press.

Governor Hunter thought it would be an excellent idea to send the Palatines upstate into the pine forests to have them make tar and pitch. Almost two thousand were sent forth, some four hundred women and children remaining in New York.

Hunter, a soldier by profession, made a poor manager as far as the manufacture of pitch and tar was concerned, so the enterprise failed. Angered by the failure, the governor refused to allow the Palatines any land for settlement. Under the leadership of Johann Conrad Weiser and Captain Kneiskern, who had headed a company in the expedition to Canada, the Germans migrated to Schoharie, where the friendly Indians gave them land. There they founded not only the town, Rhinebeck-on-the-Hudson, but also a group of villages on both sides of the Schoharie River. These were named for leaders of the Colonists: Weisersdorf, Hartmannsdorf, Brunnendorf, Schmidtsdorf, Fuchsdorf, Gerlachsdorf, Kneiskerndorf.

Weiser was a very capable leader. His son, Conrad, lived among the Mohawk Indians for a while and learned their language. He became the mediator between the Colonists and the Redskins, who traded with one another and shared festivals. On the other hand, unfortunately, the relations of the Palatines and the Dutch settlers were not as good. These Colonists, generally well-to-do patricians, were well established and looked down upon the plebeian "High Dutch."

Governor Hunter, too, was still resentful, and Conrad Weiser had to wage a long fight to maintain the rights of the Palatines to their lands. The next governor, Brunet, was more considerate and persuaded them to move to lands on the Mohawk. About three hundred remained in Schoharie; the others settled in the Mohawk Valley.

This was not only very fertile land, it was also the frontier of western New York. The Palatines, therefore, made an additional contribution to the Colony. In times of peace the area was the granary for the inhabitants; in the French and Indian War, and during the Revolution it acted as a bulwark against the enemy. In the middle of the eighteenth century there were about three thousand Palatines in that area.

Still having trouble with their landlords, a number of Palatines decided to migrate. They fixed upon Pennsylvania, since its Governor Keith had given them an invitation that promised freedom and justice. They accepted and moved in two contingents, one in 1723 and a second in 1728. About three hundred persons left Schoharie paddling canoes down the Susquehanna River. The first settlement they founded was named Heidelberg.

In 1728, the second group arrived and settled at Womelsdorf under the direction of Conrad Weiser, who was soon recognized as the leader of the Germans in Berks County. These settlements in the Tulpehocken district prospered and the people were satisfied. Their glowing reports to relatives in Europe turned the stream of immigration away from New York to Pennsylvania. Twenty years after the settlement of Tulpehocken, there were almost fifty thousand Germans in the county. Even those Germans who arrived in New York made their way through dense forest to Pennsylvania.

2. ZENGER, THE CHAMPION OF A FREE PRESS

Among the hapless Palatine orphan boys, who had been left behind in New York, was one destined to make one of the most significant contributions to freedom of thought and expression in America. That was Peter Zenger.

At thirteen years of age, he had the good fortune of being apprenticed to William Bradford, a generous, kindly English Quaker who had come over with William Penn. Bradford was a printer and had the distinction of being the only one in New York. By 1725, he had established the first newspaper, *The New York Gazette,* which did rather well. Bradford soon needed help, and he hired the young, friendless Palatine.

Zenger was a bright, diligent youth and rose rapidly—indeed, Bradford was so pleased with his work that he made him his partner. The older man was quite conservative, while the younger man was a liberal. When Bradford offered his unswerving support to the British governor, Zenger left his benefactor and started his own newspaper. *The New York Weekly Journal,* as it was named, vigorously attacked the administration and espoused the cause of the opposition.

Zenger soon found an objective for his keen, satiric pen. The new governor, Cosby, was responsible for a number of highhanded actions which the editor denounced fearlessly in the columns of his *Weekly Journal.*

His Excellency William Cosby, Captain General and Governor-in-Chief of the Provinces of New York, New Jersey, and Territories thereon depending, was filled with wrath. He directed the grand jury to indict Zenger for libel; he requested the assembly to order the public burning of copies of the *Weekly Journal.* He asserted that Zenger's vicious publication contained "divers scandalous, virulent, false and seditious reflections . . . which said reflections seem contrived by the wicked authors of them, not only to create jealousies, discontent and animosities in the minds of His Majesty's liege people of this province . . . but to alienate their affections from the best of kings, and raise factions, tumults and sedition among them."

None of the governor's efforts to silence Zenger met with success. Finally, he had the offending editor clapped into jail and held incommunicado. For ten months he remained there. On August 14, 1735, criminal procedures were instituted against Zenger. The defendant's case seemed hopeless, until the venerable Andrew Hamilton of Philadelphia came into the courtroom. This able Scotch-Irish lawyer won his case by a very simple argument: he merely pointed out that what Zenger had printed was factual, hence there was no case of libel. Despite the hostile charge by Judge Delancey, the jury returned a verdict of Not Guilty. The courtroom rang with joy and triumph. Zenger was cheered and acclaimed, and the aged and infirm Hamilton was escorted down the street by an enthusiastic crowd accompanied by a band.

Zenger possessed not only courage but also exceptional editorial skill. He made a valuable contribution to legal and historical literature by printing a verbatim account of the trial. His bail had been set so high that he had to remain in prison for almost a year. But each day his wife came to see him, and through a crack in the door he dictated articles to her. Thus, his newspaper was able to appear without interruption. Loyal employees took care of the printing.

This dramatic incident is the basis for a novel by Kent Cooper, entitled, *Anna Zenger, Mother of Freedom*. Cooper points out that, during her husband's ten-month incarceration, Anna Zenger published *The Weekly Journal* and thus became the first woman publisher in the country. She did this with skill and brilliance. According to the accepted versions, Mrs. Zenger was a pious, respectable wife and a devoted mother. On the basis of his research, Cooper concludes that she was a gifted writer—far superior to her husband. In fact, Zenger's fame is considerably diminished. According to Cooper, he was an uneducated, unimaginative, and unambitious printer. Moreover, he was incapable of writing the incisive articles and vitriolic diatribes that nettled the governor. Who wrote them? His wife—Anna Zenger.

The question may be argued, but Peter Zenger's fame will rest on his two great achievements: he founded the first independent newspaper in this country, and by his courageous stand he established freedom of the press.

3. GERMANS IN NEW JERSEY AND MARYLAND

In 1707, a number of German families belonging to the Reformed church emigrated from the Braunschweig area and set sail for New York. Driven off its course by adverse winds, their vessel landed in Delaware Bay. From Philadelphia they set out overland for New York. As they journeyed through the beautiful Musconetcong Valley in New Jersey, they were so delighted with the region that they decided to go no farther.

They settled down in what is now Morris County and eventually spread to Somerset, Bergen, and Essex Counties. The first German church was opened in 1731 near Potterstown.

A considerable number of Germans from the Palatinate also settled in New Jersey around 1710. In fact, in southern New Jersey some Germans had arrived with Swedish settlers before 1700. The inhabitants in that part of New Jersey, known as German Valley, were chiefly farmers, and through their industry and thrift converted the wilderness into prosperous agricultural areas.

A number of them distinguished themselves during the Revolutionary War: General Frederick Frelinghuysen and Johann Peter Rockefeller. The grandson of Theodore J. Frelinghuysen (or Frelinghausen), born in Lingen, Friesland, General Frederick Frelinghuysen took part in the Battles of Trenton and Monmouth Courthouse. He later became a member of the Continental Congress, of the Convention of 1787, and of the United States Senate from 1793 to 1796. The Rockefellers are descendants of early German settlers in New Jersey. In 1906, John D. Rockefeller erected a monument to the memory of his ancestor, Johann Peter Rockefeller, "who came from Germany about 1733 and died in 1783."

Although the German settlers were honest and thrifty, there was sometimes serious dissension in the churches. One of these bitter church quarrels was tactfully settled by the Reverend Heinrich Melchior Mühlenberg, the patriarch of the New Jersey Lutherans from 1757–75.

The church services were, of course, conducted in German. As time went on, however, English made rapid encroachments. Naturally there was a short transition period during which the two languages mingled. This was the case in the preaching of the Reverend Caspar Wack, who filled the pulpit of Great Swamp Church from 1771 on. An English army officer, interested in hearing what German sounded like, attended the services one Sunday morning. After listening to Mr. Wack's preaching, he exclaimed, "I never knew before that German was so much like English; I could understand a great deal of it." He had heard what was supposed to have been an English sermon!

Caspar Wack's English improved in time. To make sure of his pronunciation, he even used diacritical marks in his sermons. He was quite versatile; he conducted a singing school, ran a farm, and operated a mill. He worked from dawn to dark and grew to be quite wealthy. Later he moved to the Mohawk Valley. During the War of 1812 he served as a chaplain.

The existence of German settlers in southern New Jersey is confirmed by the diaries of itinerant Moravian preachers who knew practically no English. The Moravian settlements were noted for their cleanliness and neatness, and a model in this respect was Hope Settlement in Warren County, which boasted an unusually fine mill. This is described in detail by an admiring French soldier on Lafayette's staff, who visited it in 1778. Later, these Moravians sold their property at Hope and moved to Bethlehem.

A few Germans had settled in Maryland before 1660, having received grants of land in Baltimore County. A curious group of sectarians were the Labadists, a sect of Christian communists who settled in 1684 on the Bohemian River (now in Delaware). The founder and leader of the colony was Vorstmann, born in Wesel on the Rhine. Before emigrating, he assumed the name of Sluyter (or Schluter). With a co-worker, Jasper Danker, he was sent by the mother colony in Westfriesland to found a settlement in America. They chose the land of Augustin Herman on the Bohemian River. Herman's son became a convert to the sect. Sluyter became a successful tobacco planter and slave trader and acquired considerable wealth.

Augustin Herman was more distinguished. He was the founder of Cecil County. He had lived originally in New Amsterdam and was a prosperous dealer in tobacco. Stuyvesant sent him on various diplomatic missions. In fact, he drew a map of Maryland for Lord Baltimore which was highly praised by the King. Herman was the representative of Baltimore in the General Assembly.

Although few Germans came to Maryland before 1730, they were active in the settlement of Baltimore. Many came down from Pennsylvania. When the city was incorporated in 1796, there were three Germans among the first seven aldermen. During the Revolution, the Baltimore Germans sent several companies of volunteers. Washington's purchasing agent, Keeport (Kuhbord), was a Baltimore German. When the Continental Congress had to flee from Philadelphia, it held its meetings in a hall owned by a German merchant.

The Germans contributed greatly to Baltimore's commercial development. They engaged in the tobacco trade, shipbuilding, leather manufacture, and foreign trade. Since the city was considered so important, Bremen and Hamburg ship companies established agencies in Baltimore.

The western part of Maryland was settled by Pennsylvania Germans. The first ones, who were on their way to Virginia, arrived at the Monocacy River around 1729. They came by way of an old Indian trail which had been widened and which became the chief highway from Lancaster County to the South. The Pennsylvania Germans were particularly attracted by the generous offer of Lord Baltimore made in 1732. Families might secure two hundred acres at a rental of eight shillings a year, and individuals could rent a hundred acres on the same terms. No rent was paid the first three years.

Monocacy, the first settlement, did not last long. However, the nearby Creagerstown, founded by a German named Creager, developed. Only three miles from Creagerstown another group of Germans founded Frederick Town in 1745, the settlers consisting of a hundred families who had come from the Palatinate. Their leader was Thomas Schley, who assumed the offices of teacher and minister as well as magistrate.

These early settlements were visited by Mühlenberg, the Lutheran patriarch, and Schlatter, the leader of the Reformed. The only other Protestant denomination among the Germans were the Moravians, who founded Graceham some twelve miles northwest of Frederick Town.

Germans from the Palatinate continued to arrive in Maryland. Between 1748 and 1753 about twenty-eight hundred of them settled in Frederick or in Baltimore Counties. In 1784, John Frederick Amelung from Bremen arrived with over three hundred Germans, largely craftsmen and artisans. Their settlement, called Fleecy Dale, was on Bennett's Creek near the Monocacy. A factory for the manufacture of glass was constructed, and it attained considerable fame—Washington even mentioned it in a letter to Jefferson. In fact, Amelung traveled to Mount Vernon to present two goblets made of flint glass to Washington. When he arrived, he found a man in shirt sleeves on a ladder, fixing the grapevines. Amelung almost dropped his precious gift when he discovered that the man on the ladder was Washington himself. Amelung continued making punch bowls, wineglasses, decanters, and mirrors of a high quality.

Many settlements were founded by Germans in western Maryland. Among them may be mentioned Middleton, Sharpsburg, Taneytown, Tom's Creek, Point Creek, Owen's Creek, Union Bridge, Emmettsburg, and Woodsboro. The two settlements farthest west were Conogocheague and Hagerstown. Conogocheague was not far from the present town of Clear Spring eight miles southwest of Hagerstown. Creagerstown, a mile from Monocacy, was founded by a German named Creager.

Hagerstown was founded by Jonathan Hager, who arrived in America before 1739. He secured twenty-five hundred acres and in 1762 laid out a town which he called Elizabeth in honor of his wife. The town, however, came to be known as Hager's Town. It became the county seat and in 1807 contained over four hundred houses. Hager was elected by his district to the Assembly of Maryland.

It is interesting to note that Admiral Schley, the commander at the Battle of Santiago in the Spanish-American War, was descended from early Maryland Germans. Thomas Schley, the schoolmaster of Frederick Town, had a son, Jacob, who became a captain in the Revolutionary Army. A grandson, William Schley, was a member of Congress and governor of

31

Georgia. Several members of the family became judges and legislators.

On the whole, however, the Maryland Germans, like those of Pennsylvania, were farmers; only in Baltimore did they devote themselves to industry and commerce.

4. GERMANS IN VIRGINIA

It is generally thought that Virginia was settled predominantly by the English. In the Valley of Virginia, however, the English stock was small compared to the German and the Scotch-Irish. There were, in fact, many Pennsylvania German settlements in the Shenandoah Valley.

Like a number of other governors, Governor Spotswood of Virginia thought highly of the Germans and encouraged them to settle in his Colony. According to one report, the governor's wife was a German woman from Hanover. At the solicitation of Baron de Graffenried, twelve German families arrived in Virginia in April of 1714, to establish and operate iron works. The governor himself founded the town of Germanna. The Germans came from North Germany—that is, from Westphalia. Encouraged by the favorable reports, several other groups followed: twenty families in 1717, forty families between 1717 and 1720.

The governor pursued his pet project with energy and built homes for the Colonists. Despite these efforts, the mining operations soon ceased. The Colonists and the governor got into a dispute about who was in debt to whom, and the case was finally taken to court. Disappointed and discouraged, all but three of the German families moved away from Germanna in 1748.

They established two settlements, Germantown in 1721 and Little Fork in 1724. In both villages, schoolhouses and churches were put up. The inhabitants belonged to the Reformed faith. The German Lutherans, who had come to Germanna in 1717 and who were chiefly from Württemberg, settled in Madison County.

These settlements were on the Piedmont Plateau. The Valley of Virginia was settled by Germans coming from Pennsylvania. Eventually, a portion of the Shenandoah Valley, sloping to the north, was settled almost entirely by Germans. It is probable that as early as 1726 a number of Pennsylvania Germans founded a village, twelve miles above Harpers Ferry, which they named New Mecklenburg. In 1728, a German, Jacob Stauffer, obtained as much land as he could by counting every horse and cow as a member of his family. He settled in the northern end of the Massanutten Range and founded the town of Staufferstadt, later renamed Strasburg. Robert Harper, a German, settled in 1734 at the junction of the Shenandoah and the Potomac Rivers and founded historic Harpers Ferry, where John Brown, the abolitionist, was finally captured.

As soon as the fertility of the valley became generally known, there was a considerable influx of settlers from Pennsylvania, who not only developed prosperous farms, but also took an active part in the life of the community, establishing schools, churches, and shops. They helped to defend the frontier. In 1754, five Waggener brothers, German settlers in Culpeper County, joined Colonel Washington when he attacked Fort Duquesne.

Scattered German settlements appeared in various parts of Virginia, and there were individual Germans in almost every town. In Richmond the oldest stone house is said to have been built by a German in 1737.

Our knowledge of life in the towns and villages inhabited by Germans is based on the diaries of the Moravian missionaries who made annual trips through the frontier settlements. The earliest recorded journey of this type is that of Schnell, in 1743. The most extensive trip he made lasted from November 6, 1743 to April 10, 1744. His wanderings took him from Bethlehem, Pennsylvania, through Maryland, Virginia, and the Carolinas to Georgia. In Savannah he boarded a sloop for New York, arriving in Bethlehem five months after he had left it. The courage and the endurance of these humane and noble Moravians cannot be praised too highly, for their records have become invaluable documents in American history.

5. THE SALZBURGERS IN GEORGIA

In 1731, Archbishop Leopold of Salzburg issued a decree banning all non-Catholics from his bishopric. More than thirty thousand Protestants were driven out of their homes. After enduring many hardships, these pious, thrifty, hard-working folk were welcomed in a number of countries. About seventeen thousand of them settled down in Prussia.

Their reputation was so good that, when, in 1732, King George II of England authorized a number of gentlemen to colonize the southern part of the Carolinas, Scottish Highlanders and German Salzburgers were especially named as desirable immigrants.

General James Edward Oglethorpe left England with the first group of English Colonists and arrived at the mouth of the Savannah River on January 20, 1733. There he founded the city of Savannah.

A number of Lutheran clergymen had espoused the cause of the Salzburgers in London, forming the Society for the Promotion of Christian Knowledge. They agreed to see to it that the Salzburgers were transferred to Rotterdam. The Georgia Land Company was happy to get them and made arrangements for their transportation to America. A group of Salzburgers, under the direction of Baron von Beck, left Berchtesgaden and reached Rotterdam on November 27, 1733. Two Lutheran clergymen took over the leadership of the emigrants. They were Bolzius and Gronau, both of whom had been supervisors in Francke's orphanage in Halle.

They left England at the end of December and arrived in Charleston, South Carolina, in March, 1734. When they reached Savannah, a little later, they were received with shouts of welcome and booming cannon. General Oglethorpe was happy to have them in his Colony and permitted them to select a site for their settlement. Under the guidance of Baron von Beck, they chose a tract on the right bank of the river, some twenty-five miles above Savannah. They named the place Ebenezer, "stone of help," in emulation of Samuel of old.

A short time later, fifty-seven more Salzburgers arrived, and the Georgia Land Company generously supplied them with lumber and with tools. Thus, the little settlement took firm root. Von Beck returned to Germany to induce more Salzburgers to join the Colony. A short time thereafter, eighty more did come, together with twenty-seven Moravians and a number of English Protestants. They landed in Savannah in February of 1736.

The Moravians stayed but a brief time. When the neighboring Spaniards began to attack the settlements and armed resistance became necessary, the Moravians, who were pacifists, left Georgia and founded Bethlehem, Pennsylvania, in 1741.

On board ship with the Salzburgers and the Moravians were representatives of another religious group. These were the Wesleys—John, the founder of Methodism, and his brother, Charles. They had come to convert the Indians. John Wesley was much impressed by the humble piety and the strong faith of the Salzburgers and the Moravians. The Moravians especially influenced his religious thinking deeply. Two years later, upon his return to England, he expressed the thought in his *Journal:* "I, who went to America to convert others, was never myself converted to God." The decisive moment in his life came when he attended a meeting of Moravians in London and felt his "heart strangely warmed."

As a defense against the Spaniards, Governor Oglethorpe asked some of the Salzburgers to man a fort on St. Simon Island. Since they were loath to bear arms, most of them decided to stay in Ebenezer. A number of them, however, did go. Under the direction of their captain, Hermsdorf, they founded a settlement known as Frederica. It developed into a charming, attractive village but declined, for unknown reasons, after 1750.

Ebenezer, meanwhile, was found to be an undesirable site for a colony. The soil was not good, there were swamps, and the area was ravaged by disease. Two years after the foundation of the settlement, the Salzburgers decided to move. They chose a high ridge, eight miles lower down the river, on which they established a town called New Ebenezer.

35

The layout of the town was carefully planned. The streets were at right angles, checkerboard fashion. Provisions were made for a church, a school, a storehouse, and an orphan asylum. Around the town were pastures and fifty-acre farms. The neighboring Indians did not molest the settlers. On the opposite side of the river was the settlement of Purysburg, which had been founded by the German Swiss. Some of them came to New Ebenezer and helped build up the silk industry to promote the growing of silk. This industry so prospered that in one year the Salzburgers were able to send a thousand pounds of cocoons to England.

The settlement was a model colony; the inhabitants were thrifty, industrious, and peace loving. There were neither drunkards nor profligates. Since it was a religious community, it is not strange that it was ruled by the two pastors, John Martin Bolzius and Israel Christian Gronau. They were responsible to the Society for the Promotion of Christian Knowledge and to the Lutheran church in Germany. A code was followed which, among other things, required the support of ministers and teachers and made provision for widows and orphans. The two clergymen constituted a court which seems to have worked out very well, for not a single decision of theirs was ever appealed.

Like the Germans in the other Colonies, the Salzburgers were opposed to slavery. Most outspoken on this subject was the Reverend John Bolzius. There was, however, strong pressure of the large land-owners of the province, who needed slaves to work their plantations.

The question was finally referred to one of the superintendents of the Lutheran parent church in Augsburg. His advice was to yield, adding some pious reflections about taking "slaves . . . with the intent of conducting them to Christ. . . ." Reluctantly, the Reverend Mr. Bolzius withdrew his opposition to the repeal of the law prohibiting slavery.

Bolzius was a very capable leader and an extremely competent manager. When his colleague, Gronau, died, he continued to direct all the affairs of the Colony himself, until a successor, the Reverend Hermann Lembke, came over. Bolzius received funds from Europe which he invested in farms and industries. This income from two gristmills, a sawmill, and a rice stamping mill supplied a good income for the payment of ministers and teachers. Bolzius also promoted the silk industry. In 1733, Nicolas Amatis of Piedmont came to Georgia to instruct the Colonists in the rearing of silkworms and the manufacture of silk. In 1742, five hundred mulberry trees were sent to New Ebenezer, and a shop was established for the processing of silk.

German settlements continued to spread and grow. Farms owned by Germans were to be found on both sides of a road running from Savannah to Augusta, a distance of a hundred miles. Within a short time there were four churches in the parish, requiring additional teachers and ministers from Europe. Christopher Triebner, one of the ministers, caused dissension. However, the quarrel was tactfully settled by the Reverend Mr. Mühlenberg, the capable administrator of the Lutheran church in the Colonies (1774).

By this time New Ebenezer had attained the height of its importance. It numbered about five hundred souls who were known for their industry and sober habits. Silk was exported to Europe, and trade was carried on with neighboring towns. From New Ebenezer Germans soon spread out to other parts of the state.

6. GERMANS IN NEW ENGLAND

In certain states like Pennsylvania, Ohio, Illinois, Missouri, Wisconsin, and Texas, there was a strong concentration of Germans by the middle of the nineteenth century. In New England, on the other hand, German settlements were never numerous. The first ones were due to the efforts of Samuel Waldo.

His father, Jonathan Waldo, a Swedish Pomeranian nobleman, came to Boston as the agent of a business concern in Hamburg. He became a prosperous merchant who traveled back and forth between the Old World and the New. His son Samuel, who was born in London of a German mother, was educated at Harvard and in Germany. He was a member of the Hanoverian Elector's bodyguard when he ascended the English throne as George I. On his father's death, Waldo left London in 1724 and came to Boston. Because of his military training, he was made a colonel of militia.

Waldo was a very successful businessman. In 1732, he acquired a large tract of land on the Muscongus River in Maine, which at that time was part of Massachusetts. In 1736, a Colony was established by the Scotch-Irish on St. George's River. Anxious to get more farmers to develop the land, Waldo went to Germany in 1738 to secure Colonists. In 1740, he was able to induce forty families from Brunswick and Saxony to come to Maine. They founded Waldoburg on both sides of the Medomak River. Their lot was not a very happy one, for they were entirely unaccustomed to life in the wilderness.

Having become involved in other business affairs, Waldo turned over his Colonial enterprise to an agent named Sebastian Zauberbühler. The latter went to Germany and returned with 160 immigrants. Landing in Boston, they set out for Maine. They joined the other German immigrants at Waldoburg (Waldoboro) and suffered severe hardships. Zauberbühler stayed with them until December and then disappeared.

The wretched Colonists appealed to the governor and the Massachusetts Assembly for help. Committees investigated, debated, and reported. In the meantime, the miserable settlers had to struggle through another winter. In 1744, war broke out between England and France. The Colonists were drawn into this conflict. Samuel Waldo, brigadier-general, was third in command of the New England forces which besieged Louisbourg on Cape Breton Island. Some of the inhabitants of Waldoboro enlisted under Johannes Ulmer, while others sought refuge in nearby forts. When the war was over, they returned to the settlement.

Another disaster to befall Waldoboro, was an attack by the Indians in May, 1746. Surprising the peaceful settlement, they completely destroyed it and massacred many of the inhabitants. Those that survived returned after 1748, the year peace was concluded, to rebuild the village. Waldo, who seems to have taken renewed interest in the settlement, was able to bring twenty-five German families from Philadelphia. This brought new life into the colony; gristmills and sawmills were built, and a church was erected.

In the meantime, the authorities in Boston had become aware of the advantages of settling honest, thrifty, and hard working immigrants in Massachusetts. They were interested particularly in German Protestants who would introduce useful arts and handicrafts. In 1749, four townships were allotted for the accommodation of the prospective immigrants. Two were located in the extreme northwestern part of the state, and the other two, in the extreme western part of Maine.

A very interesting person, who helped to promote German immigration in Massachusetts, was Joseph Crellius. A Bavarian by birth, he migrated to Philadelphia and started the second German newspaper in America, *Das Hochdeutsche Pennsylvania Journal* in 1743. He became interested in immigration schemes and, in 1748, persuaded a shipload of immigrants, whom he had brought to Philadelphia, to accept Waldo's offer and settle in Maine. Concluding that there were big profits in this field, Crellius notified the General Court of Massachusetts that he would bring over German Protestants, provided there were sufficient inducements. The Court was ready to grant him two hundred acres in each township, if he was able to settle 120 Protestants within each township in three years. Crellius was not able to carry out these conditions, and so the grants were revoked.

Not disheartened, Crellius proceeded to promote his schemes with greater vigor. In his advertisements he implied that he was the authorized agent of the Massachusetts authorities and also that the British government was behind him. This caused an uproar, for by this time there were many agents interested in promoting immigration to other parts of the country. In their eagerness to make their undertaking profitable, a number of them had engaged in questionable practices, causing much suffering to unsuspecting immigrants.

However, Crellius, who seems to have been a clever fellow, dissociated himself from these disreputable agents by supporting an act—the first of its kind—for the protection of immigrants. It was passed by the Massachusetts House of Representatives in 1750. Some of the provisions forbade overcrowding on vessels and set certain minimum standards. This enraged the ship companies so much, that they refused to land in Boston.

Again, Crellius was not discouraged. In the spring of 1751, he brought over some twenty-five German families, despite efforts of his enemies to prevent his securing ships. The new arrivals landed in Boston and then proceeded to the Kennebec River. About twenty miles from its mouth they founded a settlement which they named Frankfort—the present Dresden. Among the settlers were French as well as German Protestants. Despite its name, Frankfort was not entirely German.

Immigration agents or "newlanders," as they were contemptuously called, were responsible for repeatedly deflecting streams of immigration. For example, large numbers of Germans, who would have gone to Pennsylvania or the Carolinas, were persuaded to go to Nova Scotia by John Dick of Rotterdam. Nova Scotia became a strongly German Protestant community. In 1749, a brigade of Brunswick-Lüneburg troops, who had come over in the English service, were induced to stay there by liberal offers of land. Lunenburg—originally Lüneburg—was settled by them.

From 1750, there was a steady stream of German immigration, and by 1761, more than nine-tenths of the two hundred land grants bore German names. However, in 1753, immigration to Nova Scotia was stopped by the British government, because it was felt that the country could not support more inhabitants. Waldo took advantage of this fact by making greater efforts to win the immigrants for his Maine settlements. He advertised in England and Scotland, and went to Germany with his son. Sixty families were collected, brought to Massachusetts, and absorbed in the Broad Bay settlements. Through the activity in recruiting colonists, the Germans

40

spread over a wider area. The names Bremen, Fort Frankfort, and Dresden indicate their German origin.

When Waldo died, a dispute arose about the ownership of the land. In disgust, a number of German colonists sold their holdings and migrated to the Orangeburg district in South Carolina.

The thrift and industry of the German immigrants won them a good reputation in Boston. A number of promoters decided that it would be advantageous to develop a special area for them which led to the founding of Germantown, ten miles south of Boston. New arrivals from Germany came in 1750 and in 1757. Some of the families brought over by Crellius in 1751 may have settled there. The town industrialized quickly and distinguished itself particularly through its production of glass. In 1751, Benjamin Franklin was so impressed by the prosperity of the town that he bought eight building lots there. However, by 1760, sad to relate, Germantown had declined. The colony had broken up, and many of the inhabitants headed north for the Broad Bay settlements in Maine.

4 ' The Struggle for Freedom

1. GERMANS IN THE REVOLUTIONARY WAR

Since many Germans lived along the frontier and almost constantly engaged in skirmishes with the Indians, they were prepared for the military activities later on. The first of these was the French and Indian War; this was followed by the Revolutionary War.

Of course, members of the small nonresistant sects like the Mennonites, Quakers, and Dunkards, could not take up arms in the struggle because of their religious views. They were loyal, however, and readily supplied food and clothing. In fact, in some instances, as in North Carolina, they paid a threefold tax because of their exemption from military service. It should also be pointed out that this was not from lack of courage. They had repeatedly demonstrated that they were willing to give their lives for what they believed in.

The members of the larger religious denominations, the Lutherans and the Reformed, who did not have these scruples against military service, played a leading role in the Revolution. Michael Schlatter, one of the leaders in the Reformed church, had been a chaplain in the French and Indian War and, despite his age, served likewise in the Revolutionary Army. The Mühlenbergs, father and son, were also distinguished patriots.

The Germans of Pennsylvania formed companies of militia and sharpshooters, which were sanctioned by the Lutheran and Reformed churches. In fact, in 1775, both these church groups in Philadelphia issued a pamphlet of forty pages ap-

42

pealing to the Germans of New York and North Carolina to support the enterprise. With Mühlenberg's approval the Germans of all the Colonies were urged to resist the oppression and despotism of the English government with arms. Many volunteers responded. In Pennsylvania they were known as "Associators" and met in the Lutheran schoolhouse in Philadelphia.

It is interesting to note that, on the whole, the Germans were on the side of the Revolutionaries. There were very few Tories among them in Pennsylvania. It was John Adams, who expressed the opinion in a letter to Thomas McKean, the Chief Justice of Pennsylvania, that at the time of the Revolution, nearly one-third of the whole population of the Colonies were Tories. It was quite natural that the Germans should be against the crown, for many of them had suffered in Europe at the hands of unscrupulous princes. As frontiersmen and farmers, who had carved homesteads out of the wilderness, they had developed a spirit of independence, and they certainly felt no national sentiment that bound them to an English sovereign. When Benjamin Franklin appeared before the British Parliament and was asked whether the Germans were dissatisfied with the Stamp Act, he replied, "Yes, even more, and they are justified, because in many cases they must pay double for their stamp paper and parchments." He pointed out that one-third of Pennsylvania was German.

Although the number of Tories dwindled and the proportion of Revolutionaries increased as the war went on, the Germans proved to be ardent patriots from the beginning. Many evidences of this can be cited. There were many Germans among the merchants of Philadelphia who agreed to boycott British goods. They were also well-represented in the conventions held in Philadelphia in June and July of 1774 and in January of 1775 to provide for closer relations with Massachusetts. The *Staatsbote,* published in Philadelphia by Henry Miller, later the printer of Congress, preached rebellion. In Woodstock, Virginia, on June 16, 1774, under the aegis of Peter Mühlenberg, the Lutheran pastor, resolutions were adopted challenging the right of the British government to impose taxes on the Colonists. At least half the members on the Committee of Safety and Correspondence that was organized were Germans.

But not only in Pennsylvania were the Germans patriotic; in the southern Colonies, too, they ardently supported the Revolution. In the Carolinas, for example, where the Tories often outnumbered the Revolutionists, the Germans suffered greatly because of patriotism. Of course, not all Germans were Revolutionaries. In Georgia, for instance, two-fifths of the Germans were Tories. However, in that state the Salzburgers did lend their weight to the Revolution. One of their number, John Adam Treutlen, was an ardent patriot. When the first legislative body of the state met in Savannah in May, 1777, he was elected the first governor. When his home was burned to the ground by the British in 1778, he fled and joined the army of General Wayne, serving throughout the war as quartermaster-general. There were many other Salzburgers who distinguished themselves similarly.

On May 22, 1776, Congress decided to raise a German regiment consisting of four companies from Pennsylvania and four from Maryland. In July of the next year a ninth company was added. All the officers and men were German or of German descent. This regiment took part in the New Jersey campaign; in the Battles of Trenton, Princeton and Brandywine; and spent the terrible winter of 1777–78 at Valley Forge. Baron von Ottendorff, who had come from Saxony and who had served under Frederick the Great in the Seven Years' War, recruited a corps of light cavalry in 1776. In 1780, it was merged into Armand's Legion. This regiment served in the South, in the Battle of Yorktown, and at the Siege of New York. Beside these wholly German regiments, many other army units contained large numbers of Germans. The names of hundreds of them are recorded as serving in the First to Thirteenth Continental Regiments of Pennsylvania.

In fact, Washington's own bodyguard was made up largely of Germans. Called Independent Troop of Horse, they were placed under the command of Major von Heer, who had served under Frederick the Great. Most of the men were recruited from Berks and Lancaster Counties, Pennsylvania. They began their service in 1778 and remained with the commander-in-chief during the war. Twelve of them had the honor of accompanying him to his home in Mount Vernon. Washington was highly pleased with the original troop consisting of fourteen officers and fifty-three men. Colonel John Johnson, an Irishman who came to America after the Revolution and who was well-acquainted with Washington, said that not a single man of the bodyguard understood a word of English. One may assume, then, that Washington knew some German.

Outstanding among German patriots is Peter Mühlenberg. His father, Henry Melchior Mühlenberg, was the patriarch of the Lutheran church. He sent his son to Halle, Germany, to study theology. When he returned to the Colonies, he was sent in 1772 to the Lutheran church at Woodstock, Virginia. A hearty and husky individual, the young man soon made many friends, including Patrick Henry and George Washington. He went hunting in the Blue Ridge Mountains with Washington.

Mühlenberg was made the chairman of the local Committee of Safety and Correspondence. At the state conventions in Williamsburg and Richmond he gave his ardent support to Patrick Henry. At the suggestion of Henry, Mühlenberg was made commander of the Eighth Virginia Regiment. This, of course, meant giving up his parish. When he preached his last sermon in January, 1776, the little church and the churchyard were filled with eager listeners. With eloquence he spoke of the duties of the citizen toward his country, ending fervently with the words, "There is a time for preaching and praying, but also a time for battle, and that time has now arrived." Dramatically he threw off his clerical robe and stood there in the uniform of a Continental colonel. Descending from the pulpit he marched to the open door to the roll of drums. Wild with enthusiasm, more than three hundred young men immediately joined the regiment, and the next day a hundred more followed.

Mühlenberg's men took part in most of the major engagements of the Revolution, and on February 21, 1777, he was raised to the rank of brigadier-general in command of the First, Fifth, Ninth, and Thirteenth Virginia Regiments. He distinguished himself at Charleston, Brandywine, Germantown, Monmouth, Stony Point, and Yorktown. He was Steuben's aide in creating an army.

Later on he held many important public offices. Three times he represented Pennsylvania as a member of the United States Congress, in 1789–91, 1793–95, and 1799–1801. When Franklin was president of the state of Pennsylvania, Mühlenberg was vice-president. During 1788, he and his brother, Frederick August, worked incessantly to have the Constitution adopted.

Frederick August had also been sent to Halle to study theology, but like Peter he had other interests. He entered upon a very successful political career as a member of the Continental Congress from 1779 to 1780. During the next three years he was the speaker of the Pennsylvania State Legislature and a member of the First, Second, Third, and Fourth United States Congresses. He was also the first speaker of the House of Representatives.

Another brother, Ernest Mühlenberg, who also studied at Halle, became a Lutheran minister in Lancaster, Pennsylvania. Of a scholarly bent, he was a member of the American Philosophical Society in Philadelphia and of several European scholarly associations. His son, Henry August Mühlenberg, however, was a congressman for nine years and was nominated for governor of Pennsylvania by the Democratic Party.

The Mühlenbergs continued to distinguish themselves through several generations. William Augustus Mühlenberg, the great-grandson of the patriarch of the Lutheran church in the Colonies, was the founder of St. Luke's Hospital in New York. Entering the Episcopal church, he obtained a parish at Lancaster, Pennsylvania. He helped to establish the first public schools outside Philadelphia, and in Flushing, New York, he founded a school which later became St. Paul's College. Thus, the Mühlenbergs exemplified some of the finest traits of the German-American element in America.

Of course, most of the Germans were not of the scholarly and intellectual type. Their contribution to the cause of freedom, however, was no less significant. Christopher Ludwig was an excellent example of the devotion of a middle class burgher to his country. He was poorly educated; his English was halting. But his courage was tremendous. At fifty-five he became a volunteer in the militia, having had considerable experience in military affairs. He served in the army of Frederick the Great, fought against the Turks, and spent seven years at sea.

Although he was only a baker, his tall figure and dignified bearing impressed people. He took an active part in public affairs as a member of the Powder Committee and other Revolutionary groups. In May, 1777, Congress appointed him superintendent and director of baking for the entire Continental Army. He was instructed to provide 100 pounds of bread for every hundred pounds of flour. Ludwig, however, remarked: "I do not wish to get rich by the war. I will make 135 pounds of bread out of the 100 pounds of flour." Once he had his helpers, he baked six thousand loaves of bread a day. Washington was very fond of him and called him his "honest friend." He frequently closed a toast with the words, "Health and long life, to Christopher Ludwig and his wife."

When Ludwig died in 1809 at the age of eighty-one, he left his modest estate to charity and education. Sums were to be given to the University of Pennsylvania, to two churches for the benefit of poor children, and to a committee for the founding of a free school. In Ludwig's case we have yet another example of a life of selfless devotion, integrity and patriotism. Mühlenberg and Ludwig were Pennsylvanians; the Germans in other parts of the Colonies were no less patriotic. An excellent example of a devoted New Yorker is that of Nicholas Herkimer.

The Germans of the Mohawk Valley had organized four

battalions during the summer of 1775. All four colonels were Germans; the over-all commander was Herkimer. He had been a captain during the French and Indian War and had had considerable experience in skirmishes with the Indians.

In the summer of 1777, General Burgoyne began to march down from Canada. His plan was to cut off the New England states from the rest of the Colonies. St. Leger, coming from Montreal, was to join him at Albany. When Herkimer heard of these plans, he immediately drafted all men between sixteen and sixty in Tryon County. With about eight hundred men he marched toward Fort Stanwix, which was being besieged by St. Leger. The militia under Herkimer, encamped near the present site of Oriskany, were so eager to fight that they ignored their commander's pleas for caution.

St. Leger, noting the situation, decided to prepare an ambuscade for Herkimer's men. He hid his soldiers and Indians on both sides of a thickly wooded ravine. As the Colonials made their way through the narrow road, the Tories and the Redskins broke forth from the thick brush with loud yells and fell upon them. Despite this surprise attack, Herkimer was able to rally his men and fought the Indians with knives and rifle butts. He was able to establish some order when his men reached the top of the hill. Unfortunately, at that very moment his horse was shot from under him, and a bullet shattered his leg. Seating himself on his saddle under a spreading beech tree, he calmly lit his pipe and directed the battle. The fighting continued until it was interrupted by a violent thunderstorm. In about an hour it was clear again, and the struggle was resumed.

Herkimer, whose keen gaze noted every move of the enemy, noticed that every time one of his men fired a shot from behind a tree, an Indian leapt forward to knife him before he could reload. Herkimer thereupon ordered two men to stand behind a tree, so that, while the first one was reloading, the second one shot down the approaching Indian. A bloody hand-to-hand struggle ensued, in which the Royalists were gradually driven back. Suddenly the sound of a cannon was heard

48

in the rear. A company of 250 men from Fort Stanwix attacked the British camp, capturing five flags and all the baggage. The Royalists beat a hasty retreat.

The Indians were completely demoralized. Their losses were considerable, and because of the capture of the baggage by the Americans, the Indians were not given their promised presents. From that day on they were unreliable as allies.

Herkimer's men had also suffered severely. One fourth of their number, some two hundred men, were killed or severely wounded. The greatest loss was that of General Herkimer. Nine days after the battle his leg was unskillfully amputated. He bore the pain manfully, sitting in bed smoking his pipe. He grew weaker, however, as the hours passed. When it was evident that his end was near, he asked to have his Bible brought in, and while his family gathered around the bed, he read the Thirty-eighth Psalm.

The Battle of Oriskany was a decisive victory. George Washington commented, "It was Herkimer who first reversed the gloomy scene . . . he served from love of country, not for reward. He did not want a Continental command or money."

2. A PRUSSIAN BARON DRILLS
THE CONTINENTALS

The backbone of the colonial troops consisted of common people such as the sturdy farmers of Pennsylvania and the Mohawk Valley. But the struggle for liberty also fired the imagination of a number of European aristocrats who came to the Colonies to lend their aid. The best known of these are Lafayette, Kosciusko, and Steuben.

The service rendered by Steuben was invaluable, for it was he who, in the words of Hamilton, introduced "into the army a regular formation and exact discipline," and he established "a spirit of order and economy."

Friedrich Wilhelm Ludolf Gerhard Augustin Steuben was born September 17, 1730, in Magdeburg, Prussia, the son of a lieutenant of engineers in the army of Frederick the Great. He spent his early childhood in Russia where his father had a commission in the army of Czarina Anne. It was customary then for officers to serve in the military establishments and at the courts of foreign potentates.

At the age of ten Frederick William returned to Germany with his father and continued his education at a Jesuit school in Breslau, Silesia. At sixteen he entered the Prussian army and secured a command in the infantry. He displayed such ability that he was soon a member of the general staff.

He first saw active service in the War of the Austrian Succession. In the Seven Years' War in which he was a captain, he distinguished himself at the Battle of Rossbach. He became a favorite of Frederick the Great, who made him one of his aides-de-camp (1762).

At the close of the Seven Years' War, Steuben resigned and became grand marshal at the court of the Prince of Hohenzollern-Hechingen. Financial straits forced the Prince to close his court and to live incognito abroad, and Steuben accompanied him to Montpelier, France. Later on the Prince returned to Hechingen. After having served him ten years as court chamberlain, Steuben accepted a similar position at the court of the Margrave of Baden. It was there that the title of baron was conferred on him; he was now the Freiherr von Steuben.

Having been trained for a military career, Steuben was bored by the monotony of a small provincial court. He looked about for an outlet for his military ability. His attempts to enter the Austrian army were unsuccessful. Finally, his old friend, Count St. Germain, the French Minister of War, came to his aid. He suggested that Steuben offer his services to the American Colonies.

Steuben was delighted. He met the playwright, Beaumarchais, who introduced him to Benjamin Franklin and Silas Deane, the American commissioners, who were in Paris at that time seeking support for the revolutionary cause. Steuben's ability and experience were well-known to Franklin and Beaumarchais, but they felt that an obscure baron would not cut much of a figure on his arrival in America. They decided to build him up. The clever and practical Franklin and the witty creator of Figaro furnished Steuben with letters stating that he had been a lieutenant-general in the army of Frederick the Great; they gave him a brilliant uniform with a decoration; and they provided him with a French military secretary and an aide-de-camp.

With this impressive outfit, Steuben set sail and arrived in Portsmouth, New Hampshire, on Dec. 1, 1777. In February of the next year, he was received with the highest honors by the Continental Congress, then sitting in York, Pennsylvania. Steuben, who was a cultured European, steeped in court etiquette, played his part well. He offered his services as a volunteer, requesting only a guarantee of his expenses and commissions for his two aides. Ultimate compensation would be determined later, depending upon the success or failure of the struggle. His generous offer was gladly accepted.

General Gates, who was intriguing against Washington at the time, tried to gain the Baron's favor, but Steuben's keen insight into human nature prevented his being led astray by flattery. He decided to go direct to Washington at Valley Forge. During his journey through Lancaster County, he received hearty ovations from the German farmers. On his arrival at Valley Forge, on February 23, General Washington gave the Baron and his aides a cordial welcome. Washington was impressed by his military experience and was drawn to him by his personal qualities. The two men became lifelong friends.

The morale of the Continentals was at its lowest point at that time. More than two-thirds of the original force of seventeen thousand men had been lost through death, disease, and desertion. It was a wretched lot of ill-equipped, poorly fed, and badly clothed recruits that the Baron beheld at Valley Forge. Undaunted by the depressing spectacle, Steuben immediately organized a system of inspection, selecting 120 men to form a military school. An able instructor, Steuben trained his company so well, that within two weeks the men knew how to bear arms, march, and perform maneuvers like experienced European soldiers. Within a month, all of the American troops under his inspection executed military commands with the precision of professionals. On May 5, 1778, Congress gratefully appointed Steuben inspector-general with the rank and pay of a major-general.

Steuben, accustomed to Prussian discipline, was quite impatient with the laxity, the irregularities, and the inefficiency of the men in the ranks. He insisted on meticulous attention to all details, and when his anger was roused, he swore in French and German. After he had exhausted those languages, he would turn to an officer with the plea, "My dear Jones, swear for me in English!"

The good results of his work were soon evident. His Continentals were the equals of the best British regulars. Steuben, however, was not irrevocably attached to Old World tactics. He showed his intelligence by adapting European methods to American conditions. For example, noting the topography of the country, he formed groups of light infantry who fought from behind trees and bushes in Indian fashion.

Because of Steuben's careful training, many an engagement which might have resulted in a disastrous defeat, ended in an orderly retreat. The new spirit of discipline enabled Washington to get his whole army under arms and ready to march in fifteen minutes. At Monmouth, Steuben's familiar voice rallied the broken columns of General Lee. They wheeled into line under heavy fire as if they were on a parade ground.

During the winter of 1778–79 Steuben prepared a manual entitled *Regulations for the Order and Discipline of the Troops of the United States,* which came to be known as *Steuben's Regulations* or *The Blue Book.* This excellent handbook was not only a guide to the officers in the performance of their military duties, but it also established a definite order in the requisition and management of supplies. Within one year the loss of muskets was reduced from eight thousand to three thousand.

Steuben rendered valuable service in Virginia in the winter of 1780–81 and during the Siege of Yorktown. He not only established military discipline in a general way, but created actual armies. That is precisely what he did in Virginia, where he organized an army for General Greene who had been made the commander of the Southern Army. Steuben had a real job before him: the men were ignorant of military discipline, they were demoralized, and they were inclined to plunder. Steuben frequently lost his temper in his energetic efforts to whip the raw recruits into shape. He was successful, however, and Arnold's invasion was checked.

At Yorktown his experience was invaluable, for he was the only officer who had ever participated in a siege. He was in charge of one of the three divisions when the first overtures for peace were made. He, therefore, enjoyed the great privilege of being in command when the enemy's flag was lowered.

Steuben was honorably discharged on March 24, 1784. He continued his services to his country, however, in the field where he had demonstrated the greatest ability. He formulated plans for the founding of a military academy, and one may thus say that he laid the basis for West Point. In his outline he showed that he was not merely a soldier but also a man of culture, for he stipulated that there should be professors of history, geography, law, and literature, as well as instructors in military science.

After the Revolution Steuben, who seems not to have managed his financial affairs too well, despite his organizing skill, lived for several years in straitened circumstances. Finally, in 1786, Congress granted him a tract of land, consisting of sixteen thousand acres near Utica, New York, where he took up residence. In 1790, he was voted a pension of $2500. He had also been given a gold-hilted sword in 1784.

Even in his retirement he occupied himself with matters of public welfare. Among other things he drew up plans for a system of fortifications for New York. That his educational attainments were highly regarded is shown by the fact that he was appointed a regent of the University of New York. He was the first president of the German Society of New York, which had been organized for the benefit of immigrants.

Although Baron von Steuben lacked the dramatic qualities of Lafayette, the dashing, young marquis, who shone on the battlefield, Steuben, the more prosaic German officer, made invaluable and lasting contributions to the American fight for independence. It was he who made the victories of the Continental forces possible by transforming raw recruits into trained soldiers and by instilling discipline and order in the military establishment. Furthermore, after his service in the army, Steuben became a loyal citizen of the new Republic and continued to devote himself unsparingly to its welfare.

3. OTHER GERMAN OFFICERS IN THE REVOLUTION

Another German general, who served in the army, was John Kalb. He is usually referred to as Baron de Kalb, but he was not a nobleman. Actually he was born in 1721 in Hüttendorf, Bavaria, the son of a peasant. He was sent abroad by the French government as a secret agent to gather information in the British Colonies. Upon his return he married the daughter of a Dutch millionaire and lived in comfort and in ease. In 1777 he came to America with Lafayette and offered his services to Congress. He was made a major-general and served under Washington. In the South he was given command of the Delaware and Maryland troops. Having served in the Seven Years' War and having previously visited America, he displayed great skill and acumen. He was particularly adept in matters of engineering and topography.

At the Battle of Camden General Gates had made the mistake of placing his rawest troops against the veterans of Cornwallis. The Continentals broke and ran, and with them fled Gates. Kalb valiantly continued the fight with his men from Delaware and Maryland. After his horse had been shot from under him and he had been badly wounded, he fought on foot. He led a charge and thought he had won the battle, when he was suddenly overwhelmed by a fresh onslaught of British dragoons and infantry. Kalb fought to the finish, but then had to give up because of his wounds. He lingered for three days and then died.

There were a number of other German generals—and barons—who fought with the American troops. Gerhard von der Wieden, generally known as George Weedon, was born in Hanover. He had served in the War of the Austrian Succession, in the French and Indian War and in Flanders. When the Revolution broke out, he became lieutenant-colonel of the Third Virginia Militia. In 1777, he was appointed brigadier-general, distinguishing himself at the Battles of Brandywine and Germantown. Baron Friedrich Heinrich von Weissenfels, an officer in the British Army, offered his services to Washington when the Revolution broke out. He had fought under Wolfe at Quebec and had seen that brave commander die on the Heights of Abraham. After the cessation of hostilities, he settled down as an English officer in New York. There he got married, with General Steuben as his best man. During the Revolution he defeated the British at White Plains, accompanied Washington over the Hudson, and took part in the Battles of Trenton, Princeton, Saratoga, Monmouth Courthouse, and Newton. He died in 1806 in New Orleans.

A number of other German officers came to America at the instigation of Benjamin Franklin. Among these was Heinrich Emanuel Lutterloh, major of the guard of the Duke of Brunswick, who met Franklin in London. He became a colonel on Washington's staff in 1777, and three years later he was made quartermaster-general of the army. Washington thought very highly of him. It is interesting to note that three of the most important posts in the Continental army were held by Germans: Steuben, inspector-general; Ludwig, superintendent of bakers; and Lutterloh, quartermaster-general.

Frequently German officers, intended for the British army, joined the Continental forces. Johann Paul Schott, a well-to-do, cultured young gentleman and a lieutenant of the King of Prussia and Prince Ferdinand of Brunswick, was so impressed by the struggle of the Colonies to free themselves from the British yoke, that he decided to help them. Noting the acute lack of ammunition and military equipment, he organized a supply of the needed materials. He sailed to St. Eustache in the West Indies, a Dutch possession, in the summer of 1776, chartered a schooner, loaded it with war materials at his own expense, and set out for Virginia.

In order to get by the English vessels blockading the entrance to Hampton Roads, Schott hoisted the British flag and had his crew don the uniforms of English sailors. The schooner got through, although it was fired upon by the British when they discovered the ruse. Schott ordered the Colonial flag to be raised as they entered the harbor of Norfolk, but the British uniforms, which the sailors had not had time to change, evoked a barrage of shots from the American side. A white flag was quickly displayed, the vessel was anchored, and everything was explained satisfactorily. Schott was received with joy and acclaim, and the military supplies were gratefully accepted.

In 1776, Schott was made a captain and served under Washington at New York and White Plains. At a time when many Continentals went home despite the fact that the British forces were being strengthened by fresh mercenaries from the Continent, Schott made a great contribution to the army. With Washington's permission he recruited a German troop of dragoons in Pennsylvania, appointing his own officers and giving his commands in German. At the Battle of Short Hills he was taken prisoner. Appreciating his military skill, the English commander offered him a commission in the royal forces, but Schott declined. After six months in prison he was exchanged. He served under General Sullivan, but the wounds he had received at Short Hills incapacitated him for further active service. He was made commandant of the forts in Wyoming Valley, Pennsylvania, a post that he held until the end of the Revolution. Then he settled down in Wilkes-Barre. In 1787, he was elected to the state legislature. Until his death he took an active part in public affairs.

A large number of German officers and soldiers fought in the Revolution. Many of them held important public offices after the war was over. A considerable proportion of the members of the Order of the Cincinnati—an organization of officers who had fought in the Revolution—was German. From New York alone there were fifteen higher officers, including Steuben, Lutterloh, and Weissenfels. The names of hundreds of German officers and soldiers in Pennsylvania regiments have been preserved.

Among these thousands of patriotic Germans, there are a number in whose lives there were dramatic episodes which have become part of American legend and tradition. One of the best known of these is the colorful Molly Pitcher, whose maiden name was Maria Ludwig. She was born on October 13, 1754, in Carlisle, Pennsylvania, the daughter of German immigrants. At fifteen, she became a maid in the home of Dr. William Irvine, who later served as a colonel and brigadier-general in the Colonial army.

At the beginning of the Revolution she married John Caspar Hays, a gunner in an artillery company. When she heard that her husband had been severely wounded, she set out to find him. She nursed him back to health, and then accompanied him for seven years from one battlefield to another. She helped to carry the wounded and served as a nurse. She prepared meals for the soldiers.

During the Battle of Monmouth on June 28, 1778, a very hot day, the sturdy and fearless Molly supplied the soldiers with water, carrying it in a pitcher from a nearby well. From this activity she became known as "Molly Pitcher." When her husband was overcome by the heat, she took his place at the cannon, setting it in order and reloading it. By her courageous example she prevented the vacillating men around her from retreating. After the battle, Washington personally complimented her when he reviewed the troops.

4. GERMAN TROOPS ON BOTH SIDES

In addition to the tens of thousands of Colonial Germans who served in the Revolutionary War, there were thousands of European Germans among the French troops under Rochambeau. In fact, there were entire German divisions. This was true of the first contingent, the Regiment called *Royal*

Allemand de Deux Ponts, which was under the command of Prince Christian of Zweibrücken-Birkenfeld. This regiment served in the Colonies from 1780 to 1783.

Then there were several divisions of Alsatians and Lotharingians and a battalion of grenadiers from the Saar. A number of German officers served in responsible positions in the French army. Mention may be made of Freiherr Ludwig von Closen-Haydenburg, adjutant of Rochambeau; Captain Gau, commandant of artillery; and Professor Lutz from Strassburg, the marquis' interpreter. There was also a regiment of six hundred men known as Anhalt which seems to have been composed of Germans. At the Siege of Yorktown, when Tarleton made a sortie, the English were beaten back by the Legion of Armand and the troops of the Duke of Lauzun, over half of whom must have been Germans. It is said that commands on both sides were given in German during the various skirmishes, because of the Alsatians among the French troops and the Hessians on the British side.

The Hessians have been undeservedly maligned in American history. The school texts of the past pictured them as terrible ogres, bent upon slaughtering the valiant patriots. Actually, they were a hapless lot of German peasants,—mercenaries sold to the British government by luxury-loving princes, who needed money for their palaces and their mistresses. It was a dastardly bit of business which was denounced by the fearless Schiller in his play *Kabale und Liebe*. Rosengarten presents the record of the bloody profits for the profligate princes as follows (in pounds sterling):

Hesse-Cassel	2,959,800	Anspach-Bayreuth	282,400
Brunswick	750,000	Waldeck	140,000
Hesse-Hanau	343,130	Anhalt-Zerbst	109,120

This barter in human flesh cost the British government over £7,000,000—at present values about $150,000,000. It was cruel, and it was inefficient, for the unwilling recruits, who had absolutely no interest in the war, made indifferent soldiers.

They longed for their homes and families from which they had been torn; they deserted whenever the opportunity arose. It is said that Washington was able to win the Battle of Trenton and capture all the Hessians there, because the nostalgic mercenaries had imbibed too deeply while celebrating Christmas.

In many a battle, Germans were pitted against Germans. In fact, officers, who had served under Frederick the Great, were on opposite sides, such as Steuben and Knyphausen. Some of the officers were refined, highly cultured gentlemen. This was the case of Riedesel, who was captured together with his wife at Saratoga. Thomas Jefferson enjoyed their company and their music.

After they had been captured at Yorktown, the Germans in the British army fraternized with the Germans in the Colonial regiments. When they were sent to Lancaster, Pennsylvania, and Frederick, Maryland, they received a cordial welcome from the local farmers. They seem to have been, for the most part, honest, sturdy, and thrifty burghers who were only too happy to drop their rifles and return to the paths of peace. Many of them settled permanently in Pennsylvania, Maryland, and Virginia. They became tradesmen, farmers, and even schoolteachers.

The baker, Ludwig, who himself was a Hessian, knew the character of his compatriots when he said: "Bring the captives to Philadelphia, show them our beautiful German churches, let them taste our roast beef and homes, then send them away again to their people and you will see how many will come over to us." Many of the Hessians did desert and volunteered for service in the American army.

Like other statistics about the Colonies, it is difficult to determine exactly how many Hessians remained here. Those, who stayed, settled among the German population in various towns of Pennsylvania and in Baltimore and lost their distinctive character.

An interesting tabulation of the number of Hessians in America is given by Kapp in the table on page 60.

	Sent	*Returned*	*Lost*
Hesse-Cassel	16,992	10,492	6,500
Brunswick	5,723	2,708	3,015
Hesse-Hanau	2,422	1,441	981
Anspach	2,353	1,183	1,170
Waldeck	1,225	505	720
Anhalt-Zerbst	1,160	984	176
	29,875	17,313	12,562

Of the 12,500 who did not return, one may assume that one-half survived and settled in America.

5 , America, the Promised Land

1. THE FIRST WAVE OF IMMIGRATION

At the beginning of the nineteenth century, German immigration was not very large. It ranged between two hundred and two thousand a year. Not until 1830 did it assume sizeable proportions. In 1832 it was over ten thousand, and in 1837 it was almost twenty-five thousand. These, however, are small figures compared with the numbers that came over after 1850. From 1852 to 1854 over five hundred thousand Germans reached our shores

The assumption that German immigration was slight between 1790 and 1820 cannot be verified, since immigration figures were not kept before 1820. That the numbers of German immigrants were not larger is surprising, for it had become less difficult to get to America, since the Napoleonic Wars had caused much suffering on the Continent.

It was an era of political reaction. Metternich had established censorship and espionage in the German states. Liberal student organizations and the Turner societies were suppressed. There were abortive uprisings in 1830 against the heavy taxation and the extravagance of many of the petty German princes.

Political unrest was a contributing factor to the immigration of the thirties, but economic causes predominated. The rise of the factory system threw tens of thousands of artisans out of work. Cities were overpopulated; agricultural areas were overcrowded.

In contrast to the dreary prospect on the Continent, the

United States enjoyed economic prosperity and political freedom. Rich, fertile land could be had for a low price; the West was expanding; trade and industry were thriving. Attractive offers were made by transportation companies, by land speculators, and by officials of new states eager to build up their populations. Land was cheap; taxes were low; workmen were needed. A tide of immigration began which filled not only the older settlements, but the South and the Midwest, too. The great increase came between 1830–1840.

Although most of the new arrivals were farmers and tradesmen, there were also many academically trained men among them, who were known derisively as "Latin farmers." Some of them wrote letters and articles about the new land, which were published and circulated in Germany. These reports were generally highly idealistic, and they served to stimulate the tide of immigration.

2. PANEGYRICS OF THE PEN

One of the earliest German writers on America was the distinguished scientist and explorer, Alexander von Humboldt. His scientific reports on conditions in the New World appealed primarily to scholars and intellectuals. His factual descriptions supplemented the vivid and romantic scenes depicted in the novels of Chateaubriand, who had visited the United States in 1791. It was he who wrote of America as a land of gorgeous forests and splendid streams. He influenced German poets, as well as other European poets.

In Washington Humboldt became acquainted with President Jefferson, with whom he continued to maintain a lively correspondence and an exchange of books. The German scientist met many other prominent Americans and returned to Europe with very favorable impressions of the young Republic. When King Frederick William III asked him in 1808 in Berlin what he thought of the government of the United States, Humboldt replied: "Your Majesty, it is a government which nobody sees and nobody feels, and yet it is by far mightier than the government of Your Majesty."

The early nineteenth century was a lively period for author-adventurers, particularly in the new Republic. One of these was Friedrich Gerstäcker. Restless by nature, he traveled through the wilds of Australia and America. He was a prolific writer and produced 150 volumes. The better known ones with an American background are *The Regulators in Arkansas*, *The Pirates on the Mississippi*, and *Scouting and Hunting in the United States*. He may have gotten some of his material from Reverend Klingelhöffer who arrived in 1836 from Rheinhessen and founded a settlement near Little Rock, Arkansas. Gerstäcker wrote in a lively style, but from a literary point of view his writing cannot compare with Charles Sealsfield's.

Another writer who also spent some time in America was Otto Ruppius. A number of his novels of adventure are set in the Midwest, such as *The Peddler*, *The Devil of the Prairie*, *In the West*, and *A German*. His novels did not attain the success of those of Sealsfield and Gerstäcker.

Because of the unfavorable conditions on the Continent, a number of German intellectuals developed the idea of establishing a model democratic German state in the New World. These reformers had their eye on Texas, Missouri, and Wisconsin. Two ardent young champions of freedom involved in this project were Paul Follenius and Friedrich Münch. The former was the brother of Carl Follen of Harvard. Around 1830, they expressed their plan in the following words:

"We must not go from here without realizing a national idea or at least making the beginnings toward its realization; the foundation of a new and free Germany in the great North American Republic shall be laid by us; we must therefore gather as many as possible of the best of our people about us when we emigrate, and we must, at the same time, make the necessary arrangements providing for a large body of immigrants to follow us annually, and thus we may be able, at least in one of the American territories, to establish an essentially German state . . . a territory which we shall be able to make a model state in the great Republic."

Follenius was a born leader; he was tall, impressive, tactful, and courageous. Münch, equally determined and capable, was more cautious and realistic. A society was formed which was known as the *Giessener Gesellschaft*. It drew its members largely from the grand duchy of Hessen. Arkansas was the first choice for a colony, but unfavorable reports caused the settlers to go to Missouri.

Settlements sprang up rapidly on both sides of the Mississippi around St. Louis. Many settlers of German descent lived in these communities, having come from Ohio, Kentucky, Tennessee, Maryland, and Virginia. By 1817, Missouri had sixty thousand inhabitants; in 1821, it was admitted as a state. No Germans from abroad, however, had settled within its borders.

In 1824, two Germans arrived. They were Gottfried Duden, a graduate in law and medicine, and Eversmann, an agriculturist. They landed in Baltimore and made their way via Wheeling to St. Louis. There Duden bought 275 acres of land 50 miles above the mouth of the Missouri. This was so-called Congressional land, bought at $1.25 an acre. Eversmann bought 130 acres adjoining Duden's property. A wealthy man, Duden had the land cleared and cultivated. Thus, released from all the hardships of frontier life, he sat down and wrote a romantic description of it. The book, entitled *Bericht über eine Reise nach den westlichen Staaten Nordamerikas*, was published in Elberfeld, in 1829; it was reprinted a number of times.

Duden's glowing account of life in the New World with its beautiful scenery, its unrestricted freedom, its democratic institutions, induced many a reader to leave his native land and seek this ideal existence in America. Large numbers of farmers came from Westphalia and Hanover, followed by scholars, officers, and merchants. Among them were a number of nobles, who were entirely unaccustomed to hard work. They settled in the neighborhood of Duden's farm in Warren County, Missouri. The common folk toiled hard and managed to establish successful farms. However, the intellectuals, the "Latin farmers," were in dire straits after their means of support had been exhausted, and some of them were reduced to extreme penury.

Duden was a skillful writer. Not only did he describe life in America in vivid colors, but he also contrasted it with the depressing political, economic, and social conditions in Europe. He describes the beauty of the American forest with unrestrained romanticism. He speaks of the fertility of the soil, the mild climate, the bubbling streams, the vastness of the scene. He stresses the "perfect security of person and property besides very small public taxes—these are . . . the main pillars of prosperity in America." On the other hand, he does not accept Chateaubriand's sentimental estimate of the noble Indian.

Duden's enthusiastic description of conditions in the United States made a deep impression upon his readers in Germany. In fact, it exerted such a powerful influence that Gustav Koerner, a German diplomat who came to America in 1833, published a critical review of Duden's book. Without deprecating the attractive features of the American scene, he urged readers to accept Duden's highly colored statements with caution.

In fact, as the number of immigrants increased and conditions in the New World became better known, other critics attacked Duden. He felt called upon to defend himself, and, in 1837, in a treatise on de Tocqueville's famous work, *Democracy in America,* he added a comment on his own book. He expressed regret that so many who were influenced by his description to go to America were eventually disappointed and blamed his enthusiastic portrayal. He said this was not his fault; he was misunderstood. He rejected all attacks on the America he still admired.

Duden, incidentally, was not the only one who wrote in glowing colors about the United States. Between 1815 and 1850 more than fifty books were published by Germans who had visited America. They were representative of many callings and came from various parts of Germany. Most of these reports were very favorable. For example, Tuckerman, in his book, *America and Her Commentators* (1864), remarks in comparing the German with the French and English estimates: "Some of the justest views and most candid delineations have emanated from German writers."

Among the most valuable descriptions of America are the journals of several German princes who visited the United States, Duke Paul Wilhelm of Württemberg, Duke Bernhard of Saxe-Weimar, and Prince Maximilian zu Wied. "There is hardly any work in the English literature of travel in the early decades of the nineteenth century which for kindness of tone and comprehensiveness of detail can stand comparison with these friendly and comprehensive presentations of America."

One unfavorable German work on the United States, which aroused considerable attention and which was even read by Goethe, was that of Ludwig Gall. It appeared in 1822 and was based on his experiences in 1819 and 1820. He, too, arrived with an idealistic conception of America and tells how he was disappointed. He was delighted with the scenery; he mentions the trim farmhouses, the neat farms, the impressiveness of New York Harbor, and Broadway, "the finest street in the world." He also praises parts of Pennsylvania and Ohio.

However, Gall becomes bitter when he speaks of the people, with whom he includes the German-Americans. He finds them cold, unsociable, and unkind. Making money is their chief aim in life. Again and again he thinks he has been cheated by officials and tavern keepers. In America he felt that the worth of a man depended upon his pocketbook. The press is corrupt; moral and social conditions are deplorable. But he admits that "the Americans are about a century ahead of the Germans in the efficiency of training for practical life." Many immigrants are homesick. America has not provided a better, a happier way of life.

It is significant that a number of German writers immediately took issue with Gall and asserted that he had misrepresented conditions. In his work of six hundred pages, Duke Bernhard of Sachsen-Weimar-Eisenach summarizes his estimate of

66

the United States as a "happy and prosperous country." And this was the prevailing opinion in Germany.

3. CHARLES SEALSFIELD

The most valuable literary monuments of the history of early American civilization were the novels of Charles Sealsfield. This German writer, who was proud to call himself a citizen of the United States, was the creator of the ethnographic novel. Sealsfield's writings form part of German literature. Since his works are all concerned with America and are written in English, on the basis of personal observation they may also be considered part of American literature. In fact, Sealsfield is included in the section entitled "Non-English Writings" in the *Cambridge History of American Literature*. The quality of his writing is on such a high level that Sealsfield may be called the most distinguished German-American novelist.

Incidentally, Charles Sealsfield is his pen name. He was born Karl Postl in 1793 in the little German village of Poppitz in Moravia. At an early age he entered a monastery in Prague and was ordained as a priest. Disappointed with monastic life, he fled in 1822 to the United States.

In an endeavor to forget his past completely, he pursued an entirely different kind of life and changed his name to Charles Sealsfield. Traveling widely, he journeyed through Louisiana and Texas and finally acquired a farm on the Red River. One day, as he was about to buy a number of slaves in New Orleans for his farm, his bank failed, and he lost the greater part of his fortune.

Going to New York, he devoted himself to writing. His immediate success encouraged him to attempt more ambitious works. A two volume work, descriptive of the United States, preceded a series of fascinating novels.

Sealsfield published most of his books in Germany, but they were translated and thus reached the American public. They were read with great interest; Longfellow referred to Sealsfield as one of his favorites. With consummate skill Sealsfield

67

described various American types that existed between 1820 and 1840. He was a keen observer and an interesting writer. The early pioneer, the fearless frontiersman, the wealthy southern planter, the ruthless millionaire, the bewitching society belle, the desperate outlaw, and the weather-beaten sea captain are presented in vivid colors in his novels. Sealsfield is perhaps the equal of James Fenimore Cooper and Bret Harte. In fact, he excels them in the number and variety of the types he portrays.

Sealsfield's first book, *Die Vereinigten Staaten von Nordamerika,* published in 1827 under the pseudonym of C. Sidons in Stuttgart, was such a thorough piece of work that an English version in two volumes, produced by the author himself, appeared the next year. In the first, the author treats the economic, political, social, and cultural aspects of the country; in the second, he describes his travels through the Southwest. Of this region, too, he gives a detailed account, discussing everything from the quality of the soil to life in the larger towns.

His novels fill out the picture of the New World; in all of them he displays a gift for keen perception, fair judgment, and dramatic presentation. Although he is objective and realistic, his accounts are colored by an enthusiastic appreciation of the magnificent landscape, the courageous, liberty-loving people and the free institutions of America.

In *Tokeah,* or the *White Rose,* published anonymously in English in 1828, he pictures the ruthless struggle between the advancing white man and the retreating red man. His savages are more realistic than those of Chateaubriand and Cooper.

Sealsfield visited the United States five times. His first visit lasted from 1823 to 1826. After a short stay in Germany, he returned to America in 1827 and remained until 1831. He spent the next year in England and France. By this time his fame had spread, and he was lionized in Europe with no less a person than Louis Napoleon befriending him. He settled down in Switzerland but visited the United States in 1837,

1850, and 1853. On his last visit he stayed five years. He died in 1864 on his estate, *Unter den Tannen,* near Solothurn. On his tombstone are inscribed the words *"Bürger von Nordamerika."*

While in the United States, Sealsfield traveled extensively, especially in the South and Southwest. From 1828 to 1829 he lived in Mexico. His complete mastery of French is evidenced by the fact that during the next year he was the editor of the *Courrier des Etats-Unis* in New York. He then lived for a while in Kittanning, Pennsylvania, and in Philadelphia where he was a correspondent for the German publisher, Cotta. He made many contacts with men prominent in various fields. This, together with his experiences as a planter and traveler, groomed him well for the task of portraying life in the New World.

He was deeply influenced by Scott, since he was fond of the historical novel. Sealsfield's keen powers of observation and his reduction of the romantic in his writing led to far more realistic description. His works in German were all published in Germany. His Indian tale, *Tokeah,* was written in English and appeared in America. Since he was of European origin, it is not surprising that his English is occasionally unidiomatic, but what is surprising is that Americanisms and Anglicisms creep into his German. Sometimes the author did this deliberately, in order to give exotic flavor or local color to his description.

In *Der Virey* (1835) and in *Süden und Norden* (1842) Sealsfield portrays the splendors of the tropical world in Mexico. While in Zurich, he published his *Transatlantische Reiseskizzen* which contains four novels based on life in Texas and the South. In the same year he published *Morton oder die grosse Tour* which deals with high finance, diplomatic intrigues and the aristocracy as a hated institution. In the *Deutschamerikanische Wahlverwandtschaften* (1839) he portrays social life in New York, and in *Kajütenbuch* (1841) he describes the struggle of the Texans for independence from Mexico.

69

All of these novels are distinguished by a wealth of historical and cultural material, by keen insight into various types of American character, by wonderful descriptions of the grandeur of the American landscape, and by a deep appreciation of democratic institutions. He praises the will power, the energy, the courage, and the adventurous spirit of the American. He gives them credit for concentrated reasoning and sober judgment. In *Life in the New World* one of his characters says: "There is something truly practical in our American nature that distinguishes us from other nations of the globe, —a certain straightforwardness, healthy common sense, that, unimpressed by external glitter and splendor, appreciates only real values in life; an honest, independent spirit that only pays respect to him who merits it.

"In the United States you can adopt it as a rule that so long as you act like a gentleman, you are treated as one."

After his retirement to Switzerland, Sealsfield continued to follow events in the United States with the deepest interest. With advancing years he became somewhat gloomy; he found the material progress disturbing and, as he states in *The Cabin Book*, "the political development less satisfying." Nevertheless, he praised the vigor and self-reliance of the people.

It can be stated quite definitely, however, that no European writer has ever given a more detailed, a more realistic, and a more enthusiastic picture of contemporary life in the United States.

4. A "NEW GERMANY" IN AMERICA: TEXAS

The idea of a "New Germany" in America was the conception of the ardent, young German nationalists who felt deeply frustrated by the reaction which set in after the Napoleonic Wars. When their many attempts to realize their political ideal in the Old World failed, they turned their eyes to the New World. Unfortunately, they did not appreciate the fact that the historic moment for such an enterprise had passed irrevocably.

At the beginning of the nineteenth century the emigration

which resulted in part from political conditions and in part from the change from an agricultural to an industrial economy, was uncontrolled and unguided. Because of this there was much suffering among the immigrants; there were distinct economic losses for the new land in which they settled and the old land they had left behind. However, there were idealists who thought that, by concentrating the flow of immigration to a given territory which had not yet been admitted to the Union, a German state might be established. There were also keen-witted statesmen who foresaw the possibility of economic development and the advantage of future markets in overseas German colonies.

The establishment of a New Germany in Illinois and in Missouri failed, because there were already numerous American settlements there. The best chances for the success of this idea were in Texas, since, for a short period at least, it was an independent sovereign state. Duden had drawn the attention of prospective German emigrants to Missouri; Sealsfield aroused their interest in Texas.

During the first years of the nineteenth century very few Germans settled in Texas. The earliest German settlement in that state was Bastrop on the Colorado River. In 1823, Baron von Bastrop went there with a group of immigrants, who were, for the most part, from Oldenburg in North Germany. Between 1820 and 1830 more German families settled between the Brazos and the Colorado Rivers. Although they were generally far removed from other settlers, they shared their fate and fortune. This could mean either attacks by the Indians or oppression by the Mexicans. When the Texans rebelled against the dictatorship of Santa Ana in 1836, most German males volunteered their services. They helped to gain the famous victory of San Jacinto.

In 1839, a "Germania" society was formed in New York for the purpose of establishing a German colony in Texas. As a result, a group of 130 persons set sail for Galveston on November 2. The program was a failure, however. The leaders took one glance at the forbidding wilderness and decided to return to New York, leaving their followers to shift for themselves.

Again and again, ambitious plans were made for promoting settlements in Texas. In the forties, a Frenchman, Henri Castro, founded Castroville in Medina County. Among the settlers he induced to come were Germans, Swiss and Alsatians —all German-speaking. Gradually, more immigrants arrived. By 1841 the Germans in Austin had organized a *Teutonia Orden,* which was to preserve German culture, encourage immigration, and carry on correspondence with interested parties in Germany. Through such letters and through printed reports, interest in Texas was aroused in many parts of Germany. The common folk avidly devoured the novels of Sealsfield, while the intellectuals and aristocrats read the reports of Humboldt.

One of these aristocrats, Count von Castell, an adjutant of the Duke of Nassau, suggested concentrating German immigration in one area. He interested a considerable number of minor princes and influential noblemen, who organized an Association for the Protection of German Immigrants in Texas. Each one of the members contributed a sum of money to promote the aims of the *Adelsverein,* as it was familiarly known.

Their motives seem to have been partly political, partly philanthropic. It was in the interest of British diplomacy that Texas be kept independent and that it be maintained as a sort of buffer state. Hence, German relatives of Queen Victoria and Prince Albert eagerly participated in the *Adelsverein.* Plans for attracting and aiding prospective settlers were quickly made. The Texan republic was glad to get hardworking and thrifty German immigrants, and sent agents to Europe to carry on negotiations.

In May, 1842, Count von Boos-Waldeck and Victor von Leiningen were sent to Texas to look over the land. Boos remained and founded a plantation called Nassau, while Leiningen returned to Germany with favorable reports.

The *Adelsverein* purchased a large stretch of land on the San Saba River from Henry Fischer, a native of Cassel, who had lived for a number of years in Houston. For a fixed sum the *Verein* agreed to provide transportation and give each settler a log house and 160 acres of land. A family was given double the allotment. Cattle and agricultural implements could be purchased at low prices. Moreover, the *Verein* promised to construct churches and schools and to provide medical care.

In May, 1844, Prince Carl of Solms-Braunfels set sail from Bremen with 150 families in three ships. Arriving in December, in Lavaca Bay, they were transported in oxcarts through the trackless wilderness. In March, 1845, they reached the Comal River, where Solms had bought a thousand acres of land. There a town was founded which was named New Braunfels, in honor of the prince.

The immigrants immediately set to work, and by the time a second group arrived, everything seemed satisfactory. Solms-Braunfels, however, was an inefficient manager. Dissatisfaction was so great that he resigned and returned to Europe. His successor, von Meusebach, arrived in 1845 and tried to save the situation by forced economies. This increased the dissatisfaction. In the fall of the year he rode to a spot ninety miles away where he decided to start a new settlement. This became Friedrichsburg (Fredericksburg).

In the meantime, a large contingent of immigrants had arrived at Galveston. Von Meusebach hurried there to win them for his new settlement. On his arrival he discovered that no provisions had been made for their transportation and maintenance. He hastened to New Orleans to borrow funds.

The sufferings of the twenty-five hundred immigrants were indescribable. They were huddled in tents at Indian Bay and plagued by heat, fever, and mosquitoes. Seeking work in Galveston, barons were reduced to pushing wheelbarrows. Several hundred of these wretched beings gave up all hope of getting to New Braunfels and formed a volunteer company that joined the United States Army about to invade Mexico.

Alwin Sörgel—who later published an account of the episode—and two companions did get to New Braunfels. A very strange situation prevailed. Harvests were good, and many of the inhabitants, accustomed to receiving supplies from the *Verein,* grew indolent and shiftness. Others, struck down by disease, tried to drown their misery in worldly pleasures. Every night in a hall the well and the sick joined in mad revelry to the strains of a clarinet, played by the professional gravedigger. There were so many deaths that they were piled at the door of the only physician in the settlement, the *Verein* doctor, Dr. Köster. The cemetery was jocularly referred to as "Köster's plantation." New Braunfels did not, however, disappear. During the summer of 1846 there were new arrivals who raised the morale, and the town developed into a prosperous little community.

Despite the concentration of German immigration in certain areas of Texas, the idea of establishing a German state failed. The air was filled with plans, projects, and schemes. There was even a rumor that a monarchical form of government was to be set up with the backing of British interests.

All these plans, some sober, some fantastic, collapsed when Texas joined the United States, in 1845. The representative of the *Adelsverein* in Texas, Prince Solms, the uncle of Queen Victoria, had done everything in his power to prevent the move. After the admission of Texas into the Union, the *Adelsverein* began to decline. It languished and finally dissolved in 1853.

The *Verein* had had a measure of success, however. With its support, the German immigration to Texas increased considerably. By 1850, the population of the state was about 20 per cent German, compared with 16 per cent in Wisconsin and 7.5 per cent in Missouri. Since the German immigrants were settled in compact areas, remote from American communities, Texas appeared to be quite Teutonic to the visitor of those years.

5. GERMAN CULTURE COMES TO BOSTON

With the vast increase in immigration, German influences soon made themselves felt culturally and commercially in the

Midwest. The first German church in Louisville was founded in 1838. Three years later the first lager beer brewery was opened in Milwaukee and the first German paper was printed there in 1844. In the same year the first German elementary school was opened. German concerts were given, and German plays were staged. In Buffalo a German library was established. In 1852 the first Turnverein in Milwaukee was set up.

Cultural interests kept step with economic prosperity, and by 1837, thirty-seven delegates from various parts of the country assembled in Pittsburgh to make plans for a teacher-training school and a German university. In a number of leading cities there were German book dealers.

Despite this, the German-Americans were not regarded very highly by the public. Their industry and thrift were not denied, but for certain reasons they were frequently referred to as "the damned Dutch." They were almost bound to get an inferiority complex, for visiting Germans from abroad did not regard them highly either. They deplored the low intellectual level, the preoccupation with the material things of life, and the corruption of the German language.

At the same time German scholarship was highly acclaimed, especially in New England. Madame de Staël's famous work on Germany was translated into English in 1814 and was eagerly read in Boston. Stirred by Madame de Staël's enthusiastic portrayal of work of the German universities, George Ticknor and Edward Everett went abroad in 1815 to study at the University of Göttingen. They were the forerunners of a movement which kept gaining in volume. Between 1815 and 1850 several hundred American students went to the Universities of Göttingen, Berlin, Halle, and Leipzig. Beside Ticknor and Everett, they included such distinguished names as George Bancroft, William Emerson, H. W. Longfellow, J. L. Motley, B. J. Gildersleeve, and W. D. Whitney. Of 225 American students at German universities, 137 became professors at American colleges. Bancroft, together with Cogswell, founded the Round Hill School in 1823 near Northampton, Massachusetts. It was there that the newer German ideas of elementary education, which had been observed in practice at the Schools of Pestalozzi and Fellenberg, were introduced.

Two brilliant German scholars served as teachers at Round Hill. These were Carl Follen and Carl Beck who had arrived in 1824. Beck served as a teacher of Latin, and he was also instrumental in introducing the first gymnasium in an American school.

Carl Follen soon received a call to Harvard where he became the first professor of German. He taught the language with great skill and built up an interest in the literature. By 1831, a good many cultured people in Boston could speak and read German. Despite Follen's success as a teacher his appointment was not renewed until 1836 because of his denunciation of slavery. Public opinion and the press were opposed to abolition, and Follen became unpopular. He was not only a teacher of German, but also a brilliant orator, lecturing on philosophy and ethics at Harvard. Through the influence of William Ellery Channing and Theodore Parker, he became a Unitarian minister. He served congregations in New York and in Boston, but continued his lectures on German literature and philosophy. He lost his life in 1840 when the steamer on which he was traveling from New York to Boston went up in flames.

Although Follen and Beck were scholars, they were neither bookworms nor pedants. They were enthusiastically in favor of training the body together with the mind. Follen, together with Francis Lieber, introduced physical training in Boston. Lieber had come to America in 1827. Born in Berlin, in 1800, he had taken part in the campaigns against Napoleon, including the Battle of Waterloo. Because of his verse and prose on the subject of political freedom, he was suspended from the University of Berlin. So he went to Jena and got his doctorate there in 1820. Filled with enthusiasm for the Greek revolt, he went to Greece to fight for freedom. After many hardships he sailed to Italy. Entirely without funds, he was compelled to make his way on foot to Rome. Penniless and in rags, he appealed to the Prussian ambassador, the famous historian of ancient Rome, Georg Niebuhr, for help. This generous scholar engaged Lieber as a tutor for his son and provided for him for over a year. When Lieber decided to return to Berlin, Niebuhr exerted his influence in his behalf. Despite this, Lieber was thrown into prison. Upon his release in 1825, he went to London and then to America.

With letters from Niebuhr he was introduced to scholarly circles in Boston. He wrote articles on history, biography, political science, and penology. His American adaptation and translation of the *Brockhaus Konversations-Lexikon* became the basis for the *American Encyclopedia* published later by Appleton. In 1833, he prepared curricula for Girard College in Philadelphia, and two years later he secured the post of Professor of History and Political Economy in South Carolina College, Columbus, South Carolina.

In his leisure moments he devoted himself to international law, producing volumes which gained him world-wide fame. He also became well-known through his *Manual of Political Ethics* and *Civil Liberty and Self-Government*. He wrote English as if it were his native tongue. The titles of some of his essays reveal his wide range of interests: *Essays on Property and Labor, The Necessity for Continuous Self-Culture, Penal Laws and the Penitentiary System,* and *On Questions of the Post Office and Postal Reforms.*

In 1856 he was called to the chair of political science at Columbia University. During the Civil War he was often in Washington to advise Lincoln and Stanton on questions of international law. At the request of the president he prepared the *Code of War for the Government of the Armies of the United States in the Field.* This treatise was published as General Orders No. 100 by the War Department. Lieber, who had warned southerners against secession from the start, felt the tragedy of the war sharply in his own family. Two of his sons were in the Union armies, while another one, who had married a southern girl, died as a soldier for the Confederacy.

Lieber visited Germany in 1844 and 1848. King Frederick William IV offered the man who had been lodged in a Prussian jail a few years before the supervision of all of the prisons in the kingdom. Lieber, however, declined. He was a cheerful, stimulating, and wholesome personality, an ardent gymnast and a scholarly student. He worked unceasingly for the welfare of humanity and the good of his country. At the time of his death, October 2, 1872, he was in charge of the adjudication of Mexican claims. Throughout his life he exemplified the ideals contained in the Latin verse he had chosen as his motto: "Patria cara, carior libertas, veritas carissima"—"My country is dear to me, liberty is dearer, truth is the dearest of all."

6. A CONFEDERATE GERMAN

When the Mexican War broke out, the Germans were among the first to volunteer their services from such diverse areas as Missouri, Kentucky, New Orleans, Cincinnati, and Texas. The first regiment organized in Cincinnati was entirely German. Belleville, Illinois, raised a German company. James L. Kemper, the governor of Virginia from 1873 to 1878, was a captain of volunteers in the Mexican War.

As in the Revolution and the Civil War, a number of Germans, trained abroad, rendered valuable service. Among these was Captain Henry Koch. Born in Bayreuth, he came to America in 1832 and established a colony in Clayton County, Iowa.

A more distinguished officer was General August V. Kautz, who was born in Baden, in 1828. He enlisted in the First Iowa Regiment. He also served later in the Civil War, where he distinguished himself through his cavalry raids in southern Virginia, in 1864. Another officer, who served in both wars, was Samuel P. Heintzelman, a graduate of West Point. He was a captain in the Mexican War. In the Civil War he participated in the Battles of Alexandria, Bull Run, Uniontown, Hamburg, and Fair Oaks. He was retired in 1864 with the rank of major-general.

Outstanding among the Germans who took part in the Mexican War was John A. Quitman. His father, Dr. Quitman, who settled first in Schoharie, was pastor of the Lutheran

Church in Rhinebeck, New York, for twenty-five years. John Anthony became a teacher and then studied law. Later he migrated to Ohio. In 1821 he decided to go to the Southwest. In Natchez, Mississippi, he established a successful law practice and married the daughter of a wealthy planter. As a man of unusually strong physique, he took a keen interest in athletics, particularly riflery. One of his townsmen was John Hawkins, a veteran frontiersman and owner of the famous rifle, "Brown Bess." Quitman challenged him to a shooting match and won three times.

With his reputation as a lawyer and his wealth as a planter, Quitman easily became president of the Mississippi State Senate. He was also commander of the state militia. When Santa Ana invaded Texas in 1836, Quitman organized a company of recruits and crossed the Sabine River. At St. Augustine he ran into a crowd of gamblers and criminals whom he had banished from Natchez. While resting on a couch in the hotel, one of the desperadoes was about to attack him with a dagger. Quitman, however, who had only been feigning sleep, managed to fend him off with his pistol. By this fearless action, Quitman gained the friendship of the outlaws.

Quitman proceeded with his company of volunteers, but when they arrived at the camp of General Houston, the Battle of San Jacinto had already been fought. That had ended the invasion. There was nothing for Quitman to do but to return to Natchez. The adventure had cost him more than ten thousand dollars.

He continued to take an active part in politics. When the Mexican War broke out, he was made a brigadier-general and commanded a brigade at Monterey, where he shared the honors with General Worth. Accompanying the troops that went to support General Scott, he led the assault on Vera Cruz. He was in command at Alvarado and helped storm Chapultepec. He was one of the most daring of the fighting generals in the war and in active combat at the storming of the Belen Gate at Mexico City. He was the first to enter the Grand Plaza the next morning, as the head of the tattered and worn troops.

Quitman's services had been so outstanding that General Scott appointed him governor of the City of Mexico. However, Quitman did not like the terms of peace that were proposed, favoring the annexation of Mexico. He felt so strongly about this that he went to Washington to argue in favor of such a measure.

During the Democratic Convention of 1846, held in Baltimore, Quitman was proposed as a candidate for the vice-presidency of the United States. In 1849, he was elected governor of Mississippi by a large majority. He served from 1850 to 1851. In 1855 he was elected to Congress and remained there until 1858, the year of his death. An ardent secessionist, he suggested the formation of a Southern Confederacy, one of the very few German leaders who was on the Confederate side.

6 ' The Winning of the West

1. THE GERMAN—A FEARLESS FRONTIERSMAN

Just as in the settlement of the Colonies, the Germans played an important part in winning the Midwest and the Far West. Many of the German pioneers were located directly on the frontier that ran from Maine to Georgia. They were accustomed to dealing with the Indians; they knew the topography of the country; and they were ready to trek into the wilderness.

The first German settlers in Kentucky came from the Valley of Virginia and from the western counties of North and South Carolina. In the Valley of Virginia the Germans were numerous; they even exceeded the Irish. In the Carolinas, too, they appear to have been as plentiful as the Scotch-Irish. Many Germans, however, also came from the midland counties of Pennsylvania.

The German pioneers were a sturdy lot, their women working in the woods and fields together with the men. They were honest and thrifty, but because of the difference in language, they generally refrained from taking positions of leadership in the community. That may explain why they have not been given adequate mention in the average American history text. They were always considered highly desirable settlers by a number of Colonial governors. No less a person than George Washington had plans to settle Germans on his ten thousand acres, south of the Ohio. In fact, he considered sending someone to Germany to recruit settlers, to whom he could promise free transportation to the Ohio and four years free rental. The Revolutionary War, however, put an end to his plans.

The frontier population was, of course, mixed; there were English, Germans, Irish, Scotch, Scotch-Irish, Huguenots, and Welsh. Under the influence of frontier conditions a new gaunt and sinewy type evolved, inured to fatigue and hardships.

2. GERMANS IN KENTUCKY

Kentucky occupied a key position with reference to the settlement of the Middle West, for the pioneers entered by way of the Ohio River and from the early settlements in Kentucky and Tennessee. At the mention of Kentucky, naturally the name of Daniel Boone comes to mind. Since he was born in Bucks County, Pennsylvania, and spoke Pennsylvania Dutch fluently, he has been claimed as a German. However, in his eighteenth year he went to North Carolina, where he lived as a farmer and hunter.

In 1769, together with several frontiersmen, Boone went on a trip of exploration through the forests between the Ohio and the Tennessee and Cumberland Rivers. Upon his return after two years, he returned with his wife, children, and relatives, and five other families, only to be driven back by Indians to the Clinch River. In 1775, he brought his family to a stockade on the Kentucky River, called Boonesborough. A number of other fortified settlements were established, since the Indians were hostile.

Even before Boone, a schoolmate of his by the name of Stoner (Steiner) and a companion, Harrod, had gone as far as the present site of Nashville. There some forty men, including a number of Germans, founded Harrodsburg, in 1774, the earliest settlement in Kentucky. Germans accompanied Boone on his expeditions, and German names crop up in connection with such settlements as Beargrass Creek, Hart's Station, and Lawrenceburg.

A typical frontiersman was Henry Crist (Heinrich Christ), born in 1764, in Virginia of German parents. In 1788, he set forth on a flat-bottom boat on the Ohio for the purpose of preparing salt. There were twelve armed men and one woman

82

in the company. Arriving in the Salt River, they were attacked by Indians. The lone woman was captured by the savages but later exchanged, and all the men were killed except Crist. He was so severely wounded, though, that he could not walk. Crawling on his knees with his clothes and skin torn by briars and thorns, a Negro discovered him and rode to the camp for help. Crist was found and carried to the salt camp. It took him a year to recover from his wound. Later he became prominent in politics and was elected to the State legislature and later to Congress. Despite his hard frontier life, he lived to be eighty.

Although some Germans were hunters and trappers, the great majority of them were farmers. They cultivated the land, built up the towns, and took an interest in religion and education. The first college in the valley of the Ohio, Transylvania Seminary—in fact, the first institution of higher learning west of the Alleghenies—received its first charter in 1780. In 1792, it was located at Lexington, and in 1798, it was named Transylvania University. Among the first trustees were John Bowman (Baumann), George Muter, and Jacob Froman, all of German origin.

Among the pioneers, there were also several German Jews who made notable contributions. There was Joseph Simon who set up a shop in Lancaster, Pennsylvania, before 1740, supplying the backwoodsmen with all sorts of necessities. He soon became one of the foremost Indian traders of the time. His boats went down the Ohio River, and his pack trains went across the plains. As one of the largest landholders in the Midwest, he became vitally interested in the promotion of settlements.

The brothers Barnard and Michael Gratz from Langendorf, Silesia, engaged in the import trade, after having received a business education in the firm of their uncle, Solomon Henry. Their vessels plied from Mobile to Halifax. Later they became interested in the Virginia western movement and in the attempts at reorganizing the settlements along the Ohio and Mississippi Rivers. They supplied the settlers with provisions and traded for furs with the Indians. Benjamin Gratz, the son of Michael, became a trustee and patron of Transylvania University. He was also one of the promoters, the director, and the second president of the first railroad west of the Alleghenies, the Lexington and Ohio Railroad.

Germans continued to spread into all the settlements of Kentucky. As the name implies, Frankfort was settled by former residents of Frankfurt am Main. It is said to have been a particularly gay town with a billiard table and a theater. However, the attempt to establish a library met with failure!

The central and the western portions of the Blue Grass region were also settled by German farmers. The glowing reports of the fertility of the soil attracted many settlers from North Carolina and Virginia. However, the wave of immigration was not very large until after the Louisiana Purchase in 1803, and then a much greater number of pioneers entered Tennessee as well as Kentucky.

3. GERMANS IN OHIO

The territory north of the Ohio was not settled as early as Kentucky and Tennessee, since it was inaccessible and inhabited by unfriendly Indian tribes. The first two Germans to get into the Ohio country were Conrad Weiser and Christian Post, both well-acquainted with the Indians. Weiser was mentioned previously as the son of the leader of the Palatines, Johann Conrad Weiser, and Post was a Moravian missionary.

Weiser had not only acquired a knowledge of the Mohawk language and of several dialects, but he had also won the confidence of the Indians. For this reason he was invaluable as an interpreter and an intermediary. In 1737, he undertook a journey to Onondaga in New York at the request of the governors of Pennsylvania and Virginia. He wanted to persuade the chiefs of the Six Nations to make an alliance with the Cherokees and the Catawbas of the South. His mission was successful.

In 1742, Weiser was the interpreter for Governor Thomas

84

of Pennsylvania at a parley with the chiefs of the Six Nations. In 1745, Weiser was again sent to them as an emissary, this time at the behest of Governor Clinton of New York. He managed to regain their friendship.

Three years later he was asked by the governor of Pennsylvania to travel to Ohio. This time he wanted to keep the Indians from an alliance with the French. At the same time he noted the location and strength of the French settlements in the Ohio Valley. Successful at his task, Weiser was able to persuade the Mohawk Indians to form an alliance against the French and the hostile tribes of the Ohio in 1745. Weiser died as a lieutenant during the French and Indian War.

Christian Post, partially because he had married an Indian woman, maintained very friendly relations with the Indians. This was not approved of, however, by the Bethlehem church fathers, and Post was no longer permitted to serve as an ordained missionary. Nevertheless, he continued his work independently, and, in 1761, he became the first white settler in the Ohio district in what is now Stark County.

Hopeful of founding a mission for the Indians, Post induced John Heckewelder to join him. The young man first learned the Indian tongue and gave instruction to Indian children. Post began to cultivate the land and to preach to the Indians. This attempt to found a settlement in 1761 failed because of the outbreak of Pontiac's War. Chief Pontiac was a daring and clever leader; he roused the Indians and led them so successfully, that all the western frontier forts except Detroit fell into his hands.

However, another Moravian, David Zeisberger, was more successful and founded an Indian congregation on the Allegheny River at Goshocking. By 1770, the congregation had grown, and Zeisberger moved west to Friedensdorf and Schönbrunn. To help the Indians Zeisberger even went to the trouble of having a book of the Delaware language prepared. It appeared in print in Philadelphia, in 1827.

The Moravians had had great success in training the Indians in peaceful pursuits. The communities were happy and prosperous. Suddenly, at the instigation of British agents, the Wyandot Indians were induced in 1781 to fall upon and destroy the settlements. The Christianized Indians were entirely unprepared for the murderous attack, for they had been taught gentleness and nonresistance. The peaceful Indians were first driven from their settlements by the Wyandots under the leadership of the renegade, Simon Girty. When they returned, they were barbarously massacred by a group of volunteers under the command of Colonel David Williamson in March 1782.

Despite these misfortunes, the Moravians have the honor of being the first white settlers in Tuscarawas County, Ohio. Other settlements were made along the Ohio River. In fact, it was Major Benjamin Steitz, an officer of the Revolution, who founded Columbia, now within the precincts of Cincinnati.

During the Indian wars a number of Germans acquired fame as scouts and Indian fighters. The most famous of these was Ludwig (Lewis) Wetzel. His father, born in the Palatinate, had settled near Wheeling. One day while he was out hunting with his sons Jacob and Lewis, they were attacked by Indians. Lewis, who was then only thirteen, managed to escape with his brother, but his father was killed and scalped. Both youngsters swore that, henceforth, they would kill every Indian they laid their eyes on. Many tales are told of Lewis' prowess: on one occasion he is said to have killed twenty-seven Indians; on another, fifty. He was an excellent shot and absolutely fearless. His ferocity toward the Indians, however, knew no bounds. Once he killed an Indian who had a safe conduct from General Harman. Held for the crime, he managed to escape. Recaptured, he was brought to General Harman in Cincinnati. Wetzel was so popular, however, that a mob got ready to storm Fort Washington. To prevent bloodshed the judge set him free on bond.

Enraged at his treatment, Wetzel migrated to Spanish territory. At Natchez, where he regained his popularity, he was suddenly arrested as a counterfeiter and sentenced to life imprisonment in New Orleans. After spending four and a half years in a damp cell, Wetzel was released in dramatic fashion. He feigned illness and death, and his body was dutifully placed in a coffin and given to friends for burial. In the evening Wetzel emerged from his tomb, and the coffin was dropped into the river. After the Louisiana Purchase he migrated to Texas, but the imprisonment had undermined his constitution, and he died in the forest on the banks of the Brazos River in Texas.

The Indians continued raiding the settlements until they were subdued by Mad Anthony Wayne of Revolutionary fame. A treaty was made, and new settlements sprang up on the Ohio, the Muskingum, the Scioto, and the Great Miami Rivers. On the upper Muskingum, Ebenezer Zane (Zahn) from Lancaster, Pennsylvania, founded Zanesville. In payment for the land he contracted to construct a packhorse trail from Wheeling to Maysville, Kentucky. United States mail was carried over this path for the first time in 1797. In the same year Zane laid out New Lancaster, and in this town the first German newspaper west of the Alleghenies appeared in 1807, namely, *Der Lancaster Adler,* printed in Pennsylvania Dutch.

On the present site of Wheeling, Zane had built a blockhouse which was attacked in 1882 by a company of British soldiers and 186 Indians. The fact that the fort was saved was largely due to the heroism of Elizabeth Zane, Ebenezer's sister, who at the risk of her life rushed out to get a fresh supply of ammunition.

Gradually the German settlers spread all over Ohio; practically every county contained a German township. German origin is revealed in the names Berlin, Winesburg, Saxon, Hanover, Strasburg, Dresden, Osnaburg, Frankfort, Spires, Potsdam, and Freeburg. Scriptural names, such as Bethlehem, Salem, Nazareth, Goshen, and Canaan, were given to these settlements by German Moravians, Dunkers, or Mennonites. Although Cincinnati did not contain a large number of Germans in the beginning, the German population began to increase during the 1830's. In that year the German population was only 5 per cent; ten years later it had jumped to 23 per cent; by 1850, it was 27 per cent; and in 1900, it was more than 41 per cent.

4. GERMANS IN THE MIDWEST

During the nineteenth century German immigration kept growing until it surpassed all other nationalities. The Germans, like the others, migrated to the areas where land was plentiful and cheap. Hence, the bulk of the new arrivals went to the Midwest. After the Louisiana Purchase in 1803, the valley of the Mississippi was opened for settlement, but few migrants went to New Orleans. Not until after the Battle of New Orleans in 1815 did the population increase. German settlers had arrived in that city shortly after its founding in 1718. The speculator, John Law, who founded a company in Paris for the settlement of the Lower Mississippi, had sent agents through France, Germany, and Switzerland to attract prospective settlers.

About two thousand immigrants were induced to accept the free passage and free land in "the earthly paradise." When they landed at Mobile Bay, they found nothing but an unhealthy wilderness. Decimated by disease, some three hundred of the survivors settled in 1722 in Attakapas, Louisiana, where they seemed to have prospered. Some Alsatians and Württembergers also settled about twenty miles north of New Orleans.

Later on more Germans came to Louisiana, and after 1840, New Orleans numbered ten thousand Germans among its inhabitants. There were also German settlers in St. Peters, Baton Rouge, and along the Red River.

In 1836, sixty families from Rheinhessen immigrated to Arkansas, settling near Little Rock. Their leader was the Reverend Klingelhöffer, the friend of the German traveler and novelist, Gerstäcker.

St. Louis, too, became the center of distribution on the Mississippi River for the immigrants. Settlements extended north and south on the Missouri, as well as the Mississippi, the Germans having come from Ohio, Kentucky, Tennessee,

Carl Schurz, friend of Lincoln, states-
man, general, patriot, and humani-
tarian.   *The Bettmann Archive*

Frederick William von Steuben, erstwhile general of
Frederick the Great, the
drillmaster of the Continental troops.

The Bettmann Archive

Washington at Valley Forge where von Steuben took over the training of the freezing Continentals.

United States State Department

Washington Crossing the Delaware. Painted at the request of Congress by Emanuel Leutze. The men in the boat are all Germans, and the river is actually the Rhine.

United States State Department

Professor Albert Einstein, the celebrated physicist, was born in Ulm; he is world-renowned for his theory of relativity.   *The Bettmann Archive*

Ottmar Mergenthaler, the inventor of the linotype, was born in Württemberg.
United States State Department

Theodore Dreiser, the innovator of the naturalistic American novel, whose father came from Mayen on the Moselle.   *United States State Department*

Emile Berliner from Hanover invented the gramophone, the loose contact telephone transmitter, and acoustical tile and cells. *United States State Department*

Charles Steinmetz, a remarkable inventor and consulting engineer of General Electric, was born in Breslau.

United States State Department

George N. Shuster, eminent German-American who has distinguished himself as editor, writer, President of Hunter College, United States Commissioner for Bavaria, and consultant for UNESCO. *Farrar, Straus & Cudahy*

A modern Midwest farm owned by a German-American.

United States State Department

Call to pre-dawn Easter service of the Moravians in Bethlehem, Pennsylvania, which they founded in 1741.

United States State Department

George Washington Bridge over the Hudson, one of the largest, most graceful suspension bridges in the world, built by the German-Swiss engineer, Ammann.

United States State Department

Maryland, and Virginia. Strangely enough no Germans from abroad had come there by 1821, when Missouri was admitted as a state. It was Duden, the university graduate, whose enthusiastic descriptions of the beauties of Missouri attracted thousands of Germans to this area. At first peasants from Westphalia and Hanover arrived. They were followed by barons, merchants, officers, students, and clergymen, unaccustomed to hard work in the open. Again these "Latin farmers" had a difficult time of it, and many of them perished miserably.

The next large influx of Germans was due to the efforts of the *Giessener Gesellschaft,* which had been organized to concentrate German immigration on a given area. Under the leadership of Münch and Follenius, thousands of Germans settled on the north bank of the Mississippi in what is now Warren County. From here, Germans spread out to St. Louis, St. Charles, Washington, Harmann, Warrenton, and Boonville, frequently forming more than half of the population. There were Catholics as well as Protestants, but all lived in harmony. They were thrifty and hardworking people, and soon every acre of the country was under cultivation. Trim cottages and neat farm buildings dotted the landscape.

The dream of Follenius and Münch of founding a German state was not realized, but the immigrants did establish prosperous communities where they and their children lived in peace and contentment.

5. GERMANS IN THE FAR WEST

The Far West was settled rapidly after the close of the Civil War. The predominant foreign elements among the immigrants were Germans, Swiss, Scandinavians, and Russians. Among the first immigrants were the German Mennonites, who spread out in Kansas and Nebraska between 1876 and 1878. From West Prussia they had migrated to Southern Russia (because of the liberal offer made to them by the czarist government). When they heard of the wonderful opportunities in America, they decided to cross the ocean. They became successful farmers in Kansas, raising wheat, corn, rye, and barley.

They also raised fruit trees which they had brought with them from Russia.

Although the Lewis and Clark expedition in the year 1804–05 had prepared the way, no settlements were immediately attempted. Three years later the Missouri Fur Company sent some trappers and hunters into Kansas, and in 1811 there arrived from New York one of the most enterprising and successful Germans in America—John Jacob Astor.

Astor was born in Walldorf, near Heidelberg, in 1763, of poor parents. He migrated to England and came to America after the Revolution. While on board ship, a chance acquaintance drew his attention to the opportunities in the fur trade. He had brought along some musical instruments given to him by his brother in England. These he exchanged on his arrival in New York for furs which he sold in London at a good profit. Nevertheless, he continued importing musical instruments, and he became the first regular dealer in the United States. Successful speculations in real estate and government securities increased his income. In 1809, he organized the American Fur Company, through which he acquired immense wealth. Attracted by the Far West, he moved to that area.

At his own expense and at his own risk, Astor founded Astoria, at the mouth of the Columbia River. This fur trading post was so successful that it threatened the British fur monopoly. In 1813, during the war, English troops seized Astoria and named it St. George. However it was returned to the United States after the war.

Astor had been extremely successful in his business ventures in addition to fur trading, and at his death in 1848, he left a fortune of over $20,000,000. He bequeathed $400,000 to help found the Astor Library and also left $50,000 to his native Walldorf for the building of an orphan asylum.

Around 1839, a stronger current of immigration flowed toward Oregon, although the gold rush of 1848 drew away some of its settlers. By 1853, the territory north of the Columbia River was separated from Oregon and named Washington. That region, as well as Montana and North and South Dakota, did not gain much in population until the opening of the Northern Pacific Railroad.

This was the achievement of a German, Henry Villard. Heinrich Hilgard (Villard) was born in 1835 in Speyer. After studying at the Universities of Munich and Würzburg, he came to the United States in 1853, eager to enter the field of journalism. After having mastered English, he reported debates between Lincoln and Douglas, and for three years during the Civil War he was a prominent war correspondent.

In 1866 and 1871, he visited Germany and then returned as the representative of the foreign bondholders of the Oregon and California Railroad. He became the president of this company in 1875. With the aid of German capital he gained control of the Northern Pacific Railroad, completing the western extension, and thereby creating a trunk line from the Great Lakes to the Pacific. This feat made him one of the greatest railroad magnates. Despite reverses in 1883, he regained control of the Northern Pacific. The construction of this railroad, more than anything else, opened up the Northwest for settlement.

Germans took immediate advantage of the opportunities offered. Seattle, the most important city of Washington, was founded by Henry L. Yesler, a Maryland German. He was born in 1811, in Leitersburg, named for Jacob Leiter, whose descendants became the grain merchants of Chicago. Yesler, a carpenter, journeyed to Ohio and settled in Massillon. Diligent and thrifty, he soon became wealthy. As a result of the boom on the Pacific coast, he decided to go there. From Baltimore he sailed to Panama, crossed the Isthmus, and then proceeded by ship to California. The gold of California did not attract him as much as the forests of Washington, in which he saw unlimited possibilities for lumbering. In 1853, he built a sawmill on the present site of Seattle and taught the local Indians—a rather wretched lot—the art of lumbering. As soon as lumber was available, Yesler laid out streets and built homes. In the middle of the settlement he erected a huge structure of roughhewn logs, called the "cookhouse," which served for years as a townhall, storehouse, hotel, jail, and church. Settlers came in great numbers, and Seattle became a thriving community. Yesler, who had acquired considerable wealth, was the mayor and a leading citizen. His foresight and energy had laid the foundations for one of the leading industries and one of the most prosperous cities of the Far West.

6. GERMANS IN CALIFORNIA

In California, another German was responsible not only for the development of an enormous area, but also for the development of another typically Western industry—gold mining. That was John A. Sutter. Born in Baden, Germany, in 1803, and trained in a Swiss military academy, he arrived in the West in 1834. For many years he maintained a trade route between St. Louis and Santa Fe.

In 1838, he traveled with a party of trappers to Vancouver. Boarding a vessel, he went to the Sandwich Islands, Alaska, and then back to the Pacific coast. Winds drove the vessel into San Francisco Bay, and from there he went to the present site of Sacramento, where he founded a settlement which he called New Helvetia. The Mexican governor of California, Alvarado, gave him the title to his land and conferred citizenship upon him. So much confidence was placed in him that he was made the governor of the northern frontier territory of Mexico. When California became part of the United States, Sutter was appointed chief justice and Indian agent of his district. He owned vast estates; sleek cattle roamed his pastures, and golden wheat grew in his fields. He was soon the richest man in the state.

It was not only the wheat that gleamed like gold; the precious metal was in the streams and on the ground. Discovered on January 20, 1848, by John W. Marshall, overseer of one of Sutter's sawmills, the gold proved to be a curse and not a blessing to Sutter. Before he knew it, the news had leaked out and hordes of gold seekers, adventurers, and desperate characters invaded his property, devastating the land and

92

killing the cattle. As a result, the title to his land was disputed. Although Sutter appealed to Congress for justice, he never regained possession of his property. However, the state of California voted him a pension of $3000 annually for seven years and made him general of the militia, but he was no longer the proud possessor of a vast domain.

There were, of course, among the gold seekers Germans as well as representatives of many other nationalities. Largely farmers rather than adventurers, the German-Americans settled down and cultivated the land. They were particularly successful in the production of grapes and wines. The citrus industry, too, was largely developed by German-Americans.

Germans flocked into a number of Californian cities such as Los Angeles, San Bernardino, San Diego, and Santa Barbara. In San Francisco an outstanding name of German origin is that of Lick (originally Lück). James Lick, born in Pennsylvania of German parents, was the founder of the famous observatory named for him. Among the big industrialists who were German, one should mention Claus Spreckels from Hanover, the sugar king; Henry Miller, born in Württemberg, the cattle king; and his partner, Charles Lux from Baden. The latter began a slaughterhouse in San Francisco in 1857. Since they owned 800,000 acres of land, they were able to drive large herds of cattle from neighboring states practically onto their own land.

In connection with California, another very famous German should be mentioned, namely, Heinrich Schliemann, the discoverer of Troy. By the time he arrived in San Francisco in 1851, the erstwhile son of a poor Pomeranian parson had traveled all over the world, taught himself a dozen languages, and acquired a vast fortune. He liked America—where he made much of his money—and was proud of calling himself an American citizen. He claimed that he became a citizen at the time that California was admitted to the Union, although there is some doubt about this.

In any case, he was in that state during the gold rush, and within nine months he had amassed half a million dollars.

He sat, literally, in heaps of gold. In Sacramento he stood armed to the teeth, while assistants stored the precious metal in huge safes. He had hired an office in the only steel and concrete building in the city, since he was afraid of fire. And there was a fire, the huge conflagration in San Francisco. Schliemann survived it but almost died twice from yellow fever. He left for Europe where he made another fortune in the Crimean War. In 1868, he visited America again to look after his vast holdings.

Despite his business acumen and his fantastic successes in financial operations, he was at heart a scholar. He studied ancient Greek and learned it so thoroughly that he was able to write the story of his life for a German university in Greek. With a passionate devotion that verged on fanaticism and religious ecstasy, he grappled with the problem of excavating ancient Troy. Overcoming untold difficulties and hardships, his efforts were finally crowned with success. At his death in 1890, kings and queens stood at his bier, and he was buried in a marble tomb fit for a hero.

7 · Revolutionists and Idealists

1. THE FORTY-EIGHTERS

When Napoleon had been defeated at Waterloo, the nations of Western Europe heaved a sigh of relief. The tyrant and conqueror was gone; the Continent was again free. The joyful mood was short-lived, for a new despotism replaced the old. The ideals of freedom and fraternity of the French Revolution, which the troops of Napoleon had helped to spread, were swept aside. Medieval thrones were restored, and feudal privileges were renewed. It was the age of restoration, of reaction, and of Metternich. Through the skilful diplomacy of the Austrian prime minister and through censorship and repression, the masses were held in check. Year by year, however, the cry for freedom grew stronger. Revolutionaries and radicals—largely of the bourgeoisie—demanded that the privileges of the upper classes be abolished.

The first outburst occurred in Paris on February 24, 1848. Furious mobs surged into the Tuileries and displayed such determination that the aged and timid Louis Philippe sought safety in flight. The spirited duchess of Orleans brought her young son before the Chamber of Deputies to have him proclaimed king. The republican masses, however, swept into the hall, dispersed the deputies, and set up a republic.

The Revolution of 1830 had seemed so easy that it was imitated all over Europe—in Belgium, Austria, Germany, Italy, and Poland. In Germany, the uprisings were mild and were quickly suppressed. In other countries, too, the premature revolts failed. By 1848, the areas of popular unrest had not only

95

multiplied, but the republicans and socialists had gathered strength, even in the most reactionary states. In fact, one of the first uprisings took place in Vienna, the citadel of Metternich. On March 13, 1848, the liberals rose and drove the aging despot from the chancellery and from the capital.

In the other countries the desire for freedom was linked with that of national unity. In Austria, it became a cry for decentralization. The Hungarians, Croatians, Czechs, and Italians demanded self-determination. The entire Hapsburg monarchy was in danger of collapse. To save the situation a parliament was quickly organized.

The news of the expulsion of Metternich caused liberals throughout Germany to exult, and in many of the smaller capitals there were riots. In Württemberg, in Baden, and along the Rhine, peasants and tradesmen took up arms. The revolutionary movement was highly idealistic, gay, and dramatic. In fact, in some instances it took on the color and verve of a comic opera. There was much declaiming, drinking, and singing; there were parades, demonstrations, and festivals, especially along the Rhine and in South Germany.

In Berlin the situation was more serious. Even the medieval attitudes of King Frederick William IV had yielded to popular pressure as early as 1847, and a so-called United Diet was convened. It did not accomplish anything, however, and on March 18, mobs gathered before the royal palace. Blood flowed, and the king was completely intimidated. He withdrew his troops, promised to call an elected parliament, and offered to prepare a constitution. In southwestern Germany, in Baden, and Württemberg, the radicals attempted to force the issue by the use of armed might. This attempt, in which such idealists as Schurz and Kinkel took part, failed miserably. The efficient Prussian battalions easily overcame the enthusiastic but untrained insurgents. Franz Sigel—later a general in the Civil War—fled with eight thousand men to Switzerland.

The success of the revolutionaries in Berlin and Vienna, however, made it possible to hold a national assembly. A group of distinguished intellectuals, professors, and poets gathered in St. Paul's Church in Frankfurt, on May 18, 1848, to organize a provisional government. The idealists, unfortunately, could not agree and were powerless to overcome several political factors. They wrote out a bill of rights and then dispersed. In April of 1849, the liberals offered Frederick William IV of Prussia the crown of a united Germany. Being a firm believer in the divine right of kings, he felt he could not accept a crown from a group of citizens. The efforts toward German unity and democracy had failed. As one historian expressed it, the German people have never shown any talent for revolution. The revolts of 1830 and 1848 started in Paris.

While the idealists were engaged in sophisticated debates in the St. Paul's Church, the reactionaries recovered their lost ground. New revolts in Berlin and Vienna were suppressed. Every attempt at democracy was thwarted by military strength, and in Berlin an authoritarian constitution was imposed on the parliament. In Vienna a number of the radical leaders were executed, and Prince Schwarzenberg, a man of iron, resumed the traditions of Metternich. By the fall of 1848 the revolution was dead. Thousands of political exiles swarmed across the borders into Switzerland, France, Holland, and England. Many of them ultimately came to America. These were the so-called "Forty-Eighters."

These fighters for freedom cherished a double idea: national unity and political freedom. When they realized that the achievement of the first was hopeless in Germany, they clung more fervently to the second. In fact, their passion for freedom was the greater one: they were ready to sacrifice their German background to it. They were disgusted with conditions in the Fatherland; they were ready to leave it. Where could they work out their destiny?

America, the land of the free and the home of the brave! The young democracy across the ocean exerted an unusual attraction on the minds of the Forty-Eighters. Well educated, they had read widely and knew de Tocqueville and the reports of German travelers in the States. Americans had established

97

free democratic institutions. Their magnificent land was expanding and prospering. Furthermore, many of the Forty-Eighters were poetically and romantically inclined. They were fascinated by the glorious forests and the noble Indian as portrayed by Chateaubriand. Yes, America was the promised land.

It is very difficult, in fact, impossible, to provide any accurate figures of the number of Forty-Eighters that came to the United States. Many of them came as individuals. Some came for a brief first visit and returned later. At most, they amounted to a few thousand who were entirely lost in the huge wave of German immigration between 1846 and 1856. Some of the revolutionaries came before 1848; some, years later. It is their political attitude, rather than the date of their arrival, by which they can be classified.

What was the reaction of the Germans in America to what was going on in the land of their birth? It seems that the earlier German immigrants took little interest in politics. They had come here for better living conditions and were satisfied with the opportunity to provide a comfortable livelihood for their families. They relished the free air of democracy and had absolutely no use for the autocratic princes who ruled the Fatherland. German-American sentiment, as reflected in the German language newspapers and magazines of the day, was unequivocally on the side of the revolutionists. No one raised his voice in defense of kings and queens, and many editors demanded a German republic. The possible advent of a truly democratic and united Germany was hailed with elation. Emotions ran high. There were mass meetings, demonstrations of sympathy, parades, and memorial services. In New York a great *Revolutionsfest* was held. Thousands of representatives from various ethnic groups marched down Broadway to a park, where Jakob Uhl, the publisher of the *Staats-Zeitung*, presided at a huge meeting. Speeches were made in four foreign languages.

In April of 1848, a crowd gathered in Independence Square, Philadelphia, to felicitate the French Republic and to gather funds to aid the German revolutionists. When Friedrich Hecker, one of the most colorful Forty-Eighters, arrived in Philadelphia, they gave him a parade and a banquet. There were demonstrations in Baltimore, Milwaukee, Louisville, Pittsburgh, Detroit, and Cincinnati. Hecker was greeted with tremendous ovations wherever he went. His trip across the country was a veritable triumphal tour. Other ethnic groups joined in these demonstrations, particularly the Irish and the Hungarians.

The revolutionaries in Europe realized that, in addition to enthusiasm, they needed money. Noting the favorable reception which the revolution had gotten in the States, they were determined to capitalize on American support. Louis Kossuth, the leader of the Hungarian radicals, toured the country and was quite successful in raising funds. Encouraged by this, the Revolutionary Committee in London sent over the professor and poet, Gottfried Kinkel, who had been liberated from prison very dramatically by Carl Schurz. He was received everywhere with warmth, and benefits were held for the cause of German freedom.

Unfortunately, by this time—it was 1852—enthusiasm had waned. Despite Kinkel's winning personality and brilliant oratory, he collected only eight thousand dollars. He had hoped to float a loan of two million dollars.

Kinkel had been sent by the more moderate faction of the Revolutionary Committee in London. There was also a more radical branch, and they decided to send Amand Goegg, a former member of the provisional government of Baden, to America. He had a marvelous idea for raising money and for the creation of a world-wide revolution. When he arrived in Philadelphia, he founded the German Revolutionary League, which was to provide leaders for revolutionary committees in various foreign countries. If each German in the United States contributed but one cent a week, the sum of $1,560,000 could be raised in a year. Other outstanding revolutionaries, such as Karl Heinzen, Gustav Struve, Arnold Ruge, and Franz Sigel supported the plan. Unfortunately it was a complete failure, for the older German settlers were repelled by such a radical plan.

The startling and significant fact about the grandiose scheme was that these German radicals proposed a magnificent role for America as a world leader and benefactor. It was actually a plan to realize the "manifest destiny" of the United States. America was not just a nation; it was a community of free peoples where the most diverse races and religions might live in peace and harmony. Here the ideal of democracy had actually been achieved. Why bother to try to overthrow slow-witted princes and shaky thrones? It would be much simpler for the United States to expand and assimilate other nations.

The first step was to annex Cuba and Santo Domingo; next Mexico and Latin America. The suffering peoples of these backward countries would welcome American hegemony. Then would come Europe's turn. England would be "infederated" and, thereafter, the other European countries. Australia, India, and Africa would follow. Soon a magnificent democratic world state would arise.

In September of 1852, a meeting was called in Wheeling to discuss the plan. Only 16 out of a possible 1112 delegates appeared, but that did not discourage them. The leader in the discussion was Charles Goepp, technically not a Forty-Eighter. His father had migrated from Silesia in the 1830's and had settled in Bethlehem, Pennsylvania. He had presented his ideas about America's mission in a pamphlet entitled "E Pluribus Unum." Together with Theodor Poesche, a former German student of philosophy, he wrote a book in 1853, entitled *The New Rome*, published by G. P. Putnam, New York, and dedicated to President Pierce.

The authors may have been fools, but they did possess an amazing gift for prophecy. In poetic language they described technical achievements still in the distant future.

"And why should our modern steamers not have wings and a motive power to impel them forward? . . . A little alteration of adjustment and these iron ships will leave their native element and ride in mid-air.

"We are on the eve of aerial navigation . . . the balloon, which is a toy, must be discarded and then we shall have the practical navigation of the air. The airplane is fitted for universal navigation . . . why should not man fly over the poles. Aerial navigation alone will give us the victory over Russian Continentalism."

The comments on Russia are particularly interesting at this time.

"This goal to liberate the world will not be realized before a great World War which is forever seen to hang, like the sword of Damocles, over the passing joys and troubles of the hour. This great World War will break out between the forming Union and the Russian Empire . . . No political step can be taken . . . without taking into account the Russian rulers and their tricky bureaucracy . . . Europe will be first Cossack, but then Yankee. . . ."

Through his fervor and enthusiasm Goepp was able to electrify his audience.

"We demand the extension of American freedom! . . . An Empire, not of conquest and of subjugation, not of inheritance, not of international frictions and hatreds, but of fraternity, of equality, and of freedom!"

It was all very simple. Thrilled with the lofty ideal, the delegates decided to form a People's League for the Old and New World and to found a political party to further the annexation of Europe. Full of joy, determination, and beer, the delegates left for home. Within a short time the People's League died a quiet death. All that survived were jokes about the crackpots of Wheeling who wanted to annex the world. America was not to encompass the globe.

Hundreds of thousands of Germans had migrated to the United States, but no group made such an impact on the American scene as a few thousand Forty-Eighters. Although there had been some intellectuals among the earlier immigrants, the bulk of the Germans arriving in the United States before 1848 were peasants and tradesmen. The Forty-Eighters, on the other hand, were well educated; by profession, they

101

were generally teachers, doctors, lawyers, editors, artists, or musicians. It is no wonder, then, that they were able to create a sort of intellectual renaissance among the German-American element.

There were other characteristics that distinguished the Forty-Eighter from the earlier German immigrant. He usually came alone; he was unencumbered by family and baggage. If he brought anything, it was a bag full of books and papers. He did not come directly from home; sometimes he had fled from an unsuccessful skirmish or had just gotten out of jail. Before he arrived in America, he had spent some time in England, France, or Switzerland. He knew several languages, but little English. He was well-informed about political and social conditions in the United States. As a cultivated person, his chief interest was ideas and not the practical demands of life on the frontier.

It was natural that these differences caused a split between the older immigrants and the new. The former were referred to as the "Grays" (*die Grauen*) and the newcomers as the "Greens" (*die Grünen*). The "Grays" admitted that they might not have had much booklearning, but they had cleared the land and built up prosperous farms and factories. They disliked the Forty-Eighters' radicalism, their criticism of American institutions, and their sarcastic comments on the low intellectual level of the German-Americans. In short, they detested the superior attitude of these "European beer politicians."

On the whole, the influence of the Forty-Eighters was salutary on the German-Americans and on America as a whole. This was due to certain German traits which they all manifested, whether they belonged to the radical, moderate, or conservative wings of the revolution. The Forty-Eighters were primarily politically minded. They participated vigorously in the political life of their adopted land. This meant not patronage, but the maintenance of good government. With a Teutonic stubbornness they adhered to their principle, which was never sacrificed to party or personal expediency. They refused

102

to "play the game"; they disdained the Anglo-Saxon tendency to compromise. They insisted on absolute truth, although this was quite impractical in any society of fallible human beings.

In this respect they were extremely conservative. They preferred the overbearing but uncorruptible bureaucrat of Europe to the easygoing American official. One of their ideals was efficient and honest government, and no one has made a greater contribution to the realization of this ideal than a Forty-Eighter. It was through the untiring efforts of Carl Schurz that the civil service reform was finally realized.

Another major issue, on which the Forty-Eighters—and most Germans—took an intransigeant and unequivocal stand, was slavery. There, too, the Forty-Eighters manifested their logic and their combativeness. They found slavery entirely incompatible with democracy; they demanded its abolition at once. All practical considerations were brushed aside.

Having fought for the unity of his native land, the Forty-Eighter instinctively became a defender of the Union. Freedom and unity was his shibboleth. As President James of the University of Illinois pointed out in a memorial service to Carl Schurz in Chicago on June 3, 1906:

"We who love to compromise, that characteristic of the Anglo-Saxon might have tried to worry on under some kind of system by which slavery should have increased in power and strength without weakening the vigor and might of the free states. . . . Or we might have consented to a possible dissolution of the Union. . . . But the men of '48 . . . were men not bound down by any of those traditions. . . . They were men who had suffered in behalf of liberty; they were men who had staked their entire careers on the side of freedom in the great struggle between privilege and democracy . . . they saw what was right, and they planted themselves firmly and distinctly on that side with no hesitation and no wavering. . . . The influence of the Forty-Eighters at this great and critical time of our national life was . . . decisive. They turned the balance of power in favor of union and liberty."

2. CARL SCHURZ

Of all the millions of Germans who have come to America, the one whose name stands out as an example of ardent devotion, unswerving loyalty, and tireless service to his adopted country is that of Carl Schurz. His contributions to the United States in war and peace were so significant, that they helped to shape our history. His courage, his nobility of character, and his unusual ability combined to make him an outstanding political leader. If he had not been of foreign birth, it is quite possible that he might have been elected President.

Carl (originally Karl) Schurz was born on March 2, 1829, in the village of Liblar, a few miles southwest of Cologne on the Rhine. He was the oldest son of Christian Schurz, a school teacher and a farmer. Carl grew up in the pleasant rural surroundings and among thrifty, hardworking peasants. He began his schooling in the village, transferring to Brühl, a few miles away, at the age of nine. At ten, he entered the Jesuit school in Cologne.

He was an eager student, fond of the ancient classics and of German literature. His wide reading inspired him to produce original pieces in verse and prose. They were hardly outstanding, but he did display a remarkable gift for oratory. He also became deeply interested in history, and in his earliest youth developed two ideals that motivated his later actions: he wanted to help bring about a free, liberal, and united Germany; he was eager to go to America. His reading had idealized for him the land of vast forests and huge streams, of political freedom and unlimited opportunities. Thus, the desire to emigrate grew stronger with the years.

Schurz was getting along very well at school when financial problems at home compelled him to drop out. He was, however, so thorough a student that he continued studying by himself and passed the rigid final examinations with the highest ratings. He was particularly proficient in Greek. Now ready for university, he went to Bonn, not far away. At that institution, one of his teachers, the professor of literature and history, Gottfried Kinkel, exerted so great an influence on him that it determined his future career. Kinkel was a poet, an enthusiastic liberal, and a man of great personal charm. He immediately won Schurz' admiration and lifelong friendship. The professor engaged the young man as his assistant in editing the *Bonner Zeitung*, a democratic paper. Schurz wrote vigorously and spoke eloquently. At nineteen he was the leader of a German student revolutionary movement.

The people were restless. Frederick William III, who had ruled from 1797 to 1840, was an autocrat, and his son and successor, Frederick William IV, was even worse. When the news arrived of the fall of Louis Philippe and the establishment of a new republic in Paris, the more determined revolutionists were galvanized into action. Outbursts and demonstrations took place in various parts of Germany. A bloody fray in Berlin forced the king to promise a new constitution. In South Germany military units were organized, and skirmishes with Prussian troops ensued. Jubilant, Kinkel left his lecture hall and joined the revolutionaries. Schurz followed the example and also volunteered his services in the field.

The ardor of the young revolutionists did not, however, make up for the discipline and training of the seasoned troops. A decisive engagement was fought at Rastatt in Baden. When the rebels were defeated, Schurz escaped from the city through a sewer which led to the Rhine. From there he made his way to Switzerland, to which Franz Sigel—also a later immigrant to the United States—escaped with about eight thousand of his men.

Kinkel was captured and condemned to life imprisonment in the fortress of Spandau at Berlin. There he was treated with the utmost severity, even being denied permission to read or write. His wife, a woman of courage and intelligence, determined to liberate him. With untiring zeal, she collected funds and then wrote Schurz in Switzerland, asking for a man to effect her husband's escape. Schurz immediately replied that he would undertake the daring and dangerous task. He returned secretly to Germany, made careful plans, and succeeded in freeing his friend. In November, 1850, both were able to board a ship at Rostock, on which they sailed to Leith, Scotland.

The next year Schurz was in Paris. When Louis Napoleon seized power in December, conditions became uncomfortable for the young German rebel, and the French police expelled him as a dangerous radical. He lived in London for a while, earning his living teaching German. In July of 1852, he married Margarethe Meyer, the daughter of a Hamburg merchant, and in August, they set sail for America.

When Carl Schurz arrived in New York in 1852, he was like tens of thousands of others, merely an unknown immigrant, who had no profession and knew practically no English. However, because of his remarkable ability and because of the prevailing conditions on the American scene, the unknown youth of twenty-three was destined within the space of sixteen years to rise to the rank of United States senator, foreign minister, and personal friend and advisor of President Lincoln.

The Schurz family first lived in Philadelphia. After spending a year in Europe, they settled on a farm in Watertown, Wisconsin. In order to learn English quickly and thoroughly, he read extensively. He went through the works of Goldsmith, Scott, Dickens, Thackeray, Macaulay, and Shakespeare. Since he wanted to prepare for a legal career, he also read the commentaries of Blackstone.

He took a deep interest in politics and soon became prominent in the Republican Party. One ideal which stirred him deeply from the beginning was the abolition of slavery. He felt that human bondage was absolutely incompatible with democracy. Mrs. Schurz was active, too, devoting herself to educational activities. In 1855, she established at Watertown what was probably the first kindergarten in the United States. From there it spread to other cities.

Schurz studied law, was admitted to the bar, and in 1858 began to practice in Milwaukee. His chief interest, however, was public affairs. In one of the great debates between Lincoln and Douglas, he was introduced to the future president, who immediately took a liking to him. He became a popular orator.

Through his speech on "True Americanism," delivered in Faneuil Hall, Boston, on April 18, 1859, he became nationally known. With vigor, he plunged into the campaign for Lincoln, addressing a large audience in both German and English. In fact, his bilingual ability made him extremely useful for reaching the German voter. Many of the recent immigrants, although intelligent and industrious, knew practically no English and settled in communities of their compatriots where they continued using German exclusively. It may be claimed that Carl Schurz' eloquence was a major factor in bringing about the election of Lincoln in 1860. By the time the campaign of 1864 arrived, Schurz was not only an admirer, but also a close personal friend of Lincoln. As a reward for his activities on behalf of the President, he was sent as minister to Spain in 1861.

Schurz was eager to take part in the Civil War, which had already begun. In preparation for it, he devoted himself to the study of military tactics while in Spain. The situation, however, worried him, and he returned to Washington to confer with Lincoln. He was adamant in his stand that slavery must go, and on March 6, 1862, he delivered a powerful speech at Cooper Institute, New York. A few days later the President sent a message to Congress, recommending the gradual abolition of slavery in the United States.

He was so eager, however, to enter the Army, that he secured from Lincoln a commission as brigadier-general of volunteers. Since he had had only very slight military experience during the Revolution of 1848 in Baden, and since he had only recently studied military science, there was considerable skepticism about the ability of this "civilian." Almost from the start Schurz proved his competence. Two months after his first commission, he took command of a division. After the Battle of Bull Run he was promoted to the rank of major-general. He participated in many of the most significant engagements of the Civil War, such as the Battles of Gettysburg, Bull Run, and Chattanooga, and he was also with Sherman's army in North Carolina. His military service may be rated as rather high; in thoroughness and devotion it is on the same impressive level as his political activity.

Lincoln's assassination was a severe blow to him, both personally and professionally. It is quite likely that, had Lincoln lived, he would have made Schurz a member of his cabinet and would possibly have entrusted him with the realization of a generous plan of reconstruction.

Although President Johnson's relations with Schurz were not cordial, the new president felt a certain amount of loyalty to Lincoln. He, therefore, sent Schurz on a very important mission. He was to visit the South and make a survey of conditions there. With his characteristic conscientiousness Schurz made a careful study of the situation for three months. Again and again he was told that the Negro was lazy, shiftless, unreliable, and improvident. Schurz, however, was not the man to be led astray by deeply ingrained prejudices. He concluded "that the success of Negro free labor would depend not only on the aptitudes of the laborer, but also on those of the employer." The carefully prepared report which Schurz turned in was not to Johnson's liking, since he had changed his point of view in the meantime. In fact, he even tried to suppress the document. At length, it was furnished to the Senate and became generally known. In it Schurz recommended readmission of the South into the Union with complete rights and the granting of the franchise to the Negroes. Schurz considered it "the best paper" he had ever written and recorded with satisfaction that "none of those statements of fact has ever been effectually controverted."

It seemed almost as if Schurz' usefulness in Washington had ended. Released from the demands of public activity, he decided to turn to writing. Quickly he demonstrated that he had not only oratorical but also journalistic ability. He served under Horace Greeley on the *Tribune* and then became the editor of the Detroit *Post*. In 1867, he took over the large German daily of St. Louis, *Die Westliche Post*. The courage and intelligence with which he dealt with public issues, strengthened his political position. He was proposed as senator from

Missouri, opposing General Ben Loan, who was supported by the other senator, Charles D. Drake. At the crucial moment Drake made the serious mistake of attacking the Germans of the state. This gave Schurz such a distinct advantage, that his opponent left the hall in defeat. Two days after his fortieth birthday, on March 4, 1869, Carl Schurz assumed the office of senator from Missouri.

For the erstwhile immigrant youth it was a moment of great joy and satisfaction; for the idealist and reformer, it was a solemn call to duty. He wondered to himself whether he would be able to justify the honors that had been heaped upon him. He made the solemn vow in his heart "that I would at least honestly endeavor to fulfill that duty; that I would conscientiously adhere to the principle *salus populi suprema lex;* that I would never be a sycophant of power nor a flatterer of the multitude; that, if need be, I would stand up alone for my conviction of truth and right."

This policy of absolute honesty was, however, entirely too radical for the practical politicians. Repeatedly he was attacked and obliged to defend himself. Fearlessly he could assert: "I have never betrayed my principles." Dissatisfied with the reactionary policies of the Republican Party, he started the Liberal Republican Movement in Missouri, in 1870. He opposed Grant's Santo Domingo policy, his treatment of the South, and the sending of arms to Europe during the Franco-Prussian War. From 1877 to 1881, he was Secretary of the Interior in Hayes' cabinet. Throughout his career he fought for progress, justice, and good government. Among many other things he sponsored enlightened treatment of the Indians; he installed a merit promotion system; he began the development of a national parks system; and, after the Spanish-American War, he opposed the annexation of the Philippines.

There was hardly an important issue in which Schurz did not participate. Through his uncompromising denunciation of what he considered wrong, he made himself many enemies. Secret agents were hired to shadow him, to find some irregularity or indiscretion in his life. But nothing could be discovered: his private life was spotless. Aggressive, tireless and fearless, Schurz never deviated from moral principle. He fought unceasingly for the rights of the Negro, for a better civil service based on merit, for honesty in public office, for the maintenance of sound money, the humane treatment of the Indians, the conservation of natural resources, and the promotion of international peace.

He approached every issue with intelligence as well as courage. When he became Secretary of the Interior in 1877, one of the gravest problems facing him was that of the Indian. He was being exploited, robbed, and exterminated. A commission appointed by Schurz reported that the Indian Bureau was bursting with "cupidity, inefficiency, and the most barefaced dishonesty." Schurz immediately reorganized the entire department and set forth a constructive program. According to this, the Indian was to be absorbed into the citizenry of the United States and was to be treated like any other person. He believed the Indian should be educated and enter the civilized life of the white man. He inaugurated the industrial school which later became the Carlisle Institute.

Upon his retirement in 1881, he went to New York, where, for several years, he was the editor of the *New York Evening Post*. He also contributed to *The Nation* and to *Harper's Weekly*. He never relaxed his efforts on behalf of social welfare and good government, and with his death on May 14, 1906, the country lost one of its noblest citizens of foreign birth. He never lost his love for Germany, but he gave the fullest measure of his devotion to his adopted country. His idealism and his patriotism were always tempered by common sense. The character of the man and his high moral purpose are best expressed in the following words: "Not my country right or wrong, but, my country: may she always be in the right, and if in the wrong, may I help to set her right."

3. GERMANS IN THE CIVIL WAR

Although absolutely accurate figures are not available, it is generally known that the Germans played a considerable role in the Civil War. The figures that do exist are, however, more reliable than those of the Revolutionary War. In 1869, B. A. Gould published a statistical summary for the United States Sanitary Commission, in which the numbers are given for the leading ethnic groups participating in the war.

The compilation was made state by state and resulted in the following totals:

Native Americans	1,523,267
Germans	176,817
Irish	144,221
English	45,508
	2,018,200

In other words, of the 2,000,000 men in the Union Army, 176,817 were of German birth. The actual number was probably closer to 200,000, for the origins of over 75,000 foreigners were unknown. Gould also points out that with reference to the number of enlistments in proportion to the population, the German average was 58,415 men in excess of the general average—far more than that of any other ethnic group.

Rosengarten lists the regiments which consisted almost entirely of Germans. He names eleven from New York, two from Pennsylvania, three from Ohio, one from Indiana, one from Illinois, and two from Wisconsin. There were also numerous volunteer regiments with three months' service full of Germans. Ten such regiments came from Pennsylvania alone.

The support of the Germans for the Union cause was significant from the start. Their most important service was rendered in the case of the largest border state, namely, Missouri. That state was saved for the Union by the large numbers of Germans who constituted one-half of the population of the city of St. Louis. The pro-Southern governor, Jackson, was deposed, and a Union man, Gamble, replaced him. In the skirmishes which were provoked, the Germans played a leading part. They organized Home Guards; German language newspapers denounced secession; German orators acclaimed the Union. The Secessionists were enraged, and pitched battles took place between them and the Germans. A bloody conflict occurred at Wilson Creek, in which General Sigel was defeated by the Confederates. However, when General Pope took command, the state was cleared of rebels.

Among the many German regiments, the Eleventh Corps contained two divisions which were entirely German and which were under the command of Steinwehr and Schurz. These divisions played a heroic part in the Battles of Chancellorsville and Lookout Mountain. General Lee had ordered the famous attack on the center of the Union forces known as Pickett's Charge. Armistead, a brigade commander, leaped on to a stone wall, waved his sword, and shouted, "Give 'm the cold steel, boys!" A hundred Confederates rushed up and planted battle flags on Cemetery Ridge. But the Union soldiers stood their ground. The defense was carried out chiefly by the divisions of Steinwehr and Schurz.

Another engagement in which the Germans distinguished themselves was that of Missionary Ridge. General Grant had commanded the divisions to move forward. They did; defying the Confederate artillery, they captured the ridge. A considerable proportion of the Union troops consisted of Germans under the command of General Willich, a native of Prussia. They were known for their courage.

The participation of the Germans in the Civil War was not only considerable in numbers, but distinguished in leadership. Some five hundred Germans with the rank of major, colonel, or general served in the Union army, and ninety-six of them were killed. Of the nine generals of German birth, seven of them were major-generals. One of these was Major-General Franz Sigel, outstanding for his devoted service, although by no means a military genius. Born in Sinsheim, Baden, in 1824, he received his military training at the Karlsruhe Academy. He entered the army of the Duke of Baden, where he rose to the rank of chief adjutant in the artillery. Having killed an adversary in a duel, and a man of pronounced liberal views, he left the army and went to Heidelberg to study law.

Together with Friedrich Hecker he took part in the revolution in Baden. The Prussians defeated the insurrectionists, and Sigel was forced to retreat to Switzerland. Although he lost the battle, he effected the retreat with such skill that there was practically no loss of men or material. In fact, his generalship won him such fame that later on in the Civil War young German-Americans were eager to serve under him.

Leaving Switzerland in 1851, Sigel went first to England and then to the United States. He supported himself in New York by teaching. In 1857, he went to St. Louis, where he taught at the German-American Institute. At that time Missouri was in a crucial position. Its governor, C. F. Jackson, had strong southern sympathies and tried to swing the state to the Confederate side. A large part of the native population tried to remain neutral. This was found to be impossible. Governor Jackson sent an appeal to the South for armed forces to seize the United States arsenal at St. Louis. However, it was saved for the Union largely through the efforts of the Germans. When President Lincoln issued a call for volunteers, Franz Sigel organized one of the first regiments in Missouri, the Third Missouri Volunteers.

In 1860, more than half of the population of 160,000 in St. Louis was German and anti-slavery. Under the leadership of Congressman Blair, the German volunteers and Home Guards captured 1,000 secessionists who were about to take possession of the arsenal. They entered the fort and armed four regiments with the available supplies. On the following morning, May 10, 1861, they surrounded and captured Camp Jackson. The governor was forced to flee for his life, and Missouri was saved for the Union. The first real battle occurred at Cole Camp, where the German Home Guards were successful in forcing the rebels to retreat. The next engagement was at Carthage, where General Sigel was in command of the Union forces. He had only eleven hundred men against the enemy's five thousand, and the outcome was indecisive.

On July 25 General Fremont arrived in St. Louis to take command. He left Lyon and Sigel in the vicinity of Springfield

113

with rather small forces. The five thousand volunteers, attacked by the twelve thousand rebels, suffered a defeat. Fortunately, McDowell did not follow up his victory, and Missouri was cleared of the Confederates when General Pope took over. Sigel retrieved his military reputation by the decisive Union victory at Pea Ridge which definitely kept Missouri within the Union.

Sigel did not distinguish himself again until the second Battle of Bull Run where he skilfully covered the retreat. On the eve of the Battle of Chancellorsville he had to withdraw for a while because of ill health. At New Market, West Virginia, in 1864 he suffered a humiliating defeat. On the other hand, he was largely instrumental in saving Washington when that city was threatened by the Confederate General, Jubal Early. Sigel detained him near Harpers Ferry for four days, thus making it possible for reserves to be rushed to the capital. Unfortunately, the defeat at New Market brought about his removal.

Sigel was immensely popular with the German-Americans, although his military achievements were not brilliant. His extreme popularity is all the stranger when one considers that he was a small, unimpressive man of cold and reserved bearing. On the other hand, his unswerving support of the ideals of democracy, his unquestioned bravery, and his ardent espousal of the Union cause won him an important place in the history of the Civil War.

Curiously enough, the military successes of the "civilian" Carl Schurz were more notable. Some of the Forty-Eighters were even jealous of his commission as brigadier-general, asserting that he was crowding out the professional soldier, Franz Sigel, their favorite. However, for everything he undertook, Schurz made careful preparations. His service in the Baden Revolution and his studies of military science in Spain had not been in vain. According to the reports of his superiors and fellow officers, he was an able commander. He showed this at the second Battle of Bull Run where his division fought in the woods before a railroad embankment for eight hours. At

Chancellorsville, he demonstrated his knowledge of military tactics by advising against placing the Eleventh Corps in a vulnerable position. Yet in the Battle of Gettysburg, his division bore the brunt of the attack, but he was able to withdraw skilfully to Cemetery Ridge. At the Battle of Missionary Ridge he was obliged to stand in reserve during the major part of the engagement.

Because of a bitter quarrel with General Hooker over a military action performed by Colonel Hecker, Schurz left the Eleventh Corps to be put in charge of a training station for recruits at Nashville. He was also active in the campaign to re-elect Lincoln. As soon as the election was over, he again entered active military service. He was serving as Chief of Staff under Sherman when the surrender came. Although Schurz was not a professional soldier, he was given the highest praise by some of his superiors and fellow officers.

The third member of the Forty-Eighters, Major General Joseph P. Osterhaus, rose to that post from the rank of private. He had had considerable military experience in Germany. After receiving his training in a military academy in Berlin, he served in the Schleswig-Holstein War. Next he took part in the revolutionary skirmishes in Baden which led to his flight to the United States. When the Civil War broke out, he was in St. Louis. Sympathizing with the Union cause, he immediately enlisted in the Second Missouri Regiment. He displayed such knowledge of tactics that he was soon made a major. A few months later he rose to colonel and helped to clear Missouri of the rebels. All of the assignments that were given him so far were of a difficult and disagreeable nature. Yet he carried them out with skill and precision.

Finally, at the Battle of Lookout Mountain he distinguished himself again. After throwing a pontoon bridge across the swollen Tennessee River, he attacked the mountain. The Confederates were put to flight, and the mountain was captured by the Union forces. He was promoted to the rank of major-general and joined Sherman in the march to Savannah.

Osterhaus took part in thirty-four battles and never met

defeat. Even the Confederates were impressed with his ability, flexibility, and courage.

Another Forty-Eighter who rose from private to general was August von Willich. He was of an old noble family with a military tradition. His father had served with the hussars in the Napoleonic Wars. Willich got his training in Potsdam and at the military academy in Berlin. At thirty, he was a captain of the artillery and could look forward to a successful military career. But his outlook on life changed and remaining a Prussian officer became impossible.

Despite his noble ancestry, he had become imbued with radical ideas. Because of a refusal to accept an assignment to a distant province, he was court-martialed. His judges were lenient; they permitted him to resign. Dropping all his aristocratic privileges, he became a carpenter. His relatives and former associates were outraged when he walked across the parade ground with an ax on his shoulder and a saw in his hand.

When the Revolution of 1848 broke out, he hastened to Baden and became a leader of the volunteers. The failure of the uprising forced him, like so many, to flee to Switzerland and then to England. Although he was an ardent devotee of communism and not ashamed of becoming an ordinary workingman, his thinking and disposition were those of an intellectual. Karl Marx ridiculed him as a "spiritual communist."

In 1853, he landed in New York, where he earned his living as a carpenter. Later he became the editor of a workers' paper in Cincinnati. When President Lincoln issued his call for volunteers, Willich joined the Ninth Ohio Regiment and immediately became an adjutant, and soon entered the West Virginia campaign. In Indiana, at the request of the governor, he organized the Thirty-second Indiana Regiment, and taught Prussian maneuvers within a month. At first there was much amusement among the troops over his stilted, literary English and his Prussian accent. Very soon, however, his skill in battle and his courage in combat gained for him the respect and admiration of all his soldiers. He fought with distinction in

116

more than thirty battles, including Shiloh, Perryville, Murfreesboro, Chickamauga, and Missionary Ridge.

At the Battle of Missionary Ridge he carried out a spectacular feat. Without waiting for orders, he had his nine regiments storm the summit. He was in the throes of combat when a bullet wound incapacitated him in May, 1864, and put an end to his active service. Nevertheless, he was made commander of the Cincinnati district and went to Texas in March, 1865, with his corps.

Although a stern disciplinarian, Willich was extremely popular with his men. He was fundamentally democratic: he never asked a soldier to do what he was not ready to do himself. Among his warmest admirers were the non-German officers who served under him. His radical ideas apparently did not interfere in the least with his effectiveness as an officer in the Union Army. Demonstrating ability and courage in all engagements, he ended his military career with the rank of major-general. Despite his many years of service in the camp and on the battlefield, he was a man of fine character and intellectual aspirations. At the age of sixty he matriculated as a student of philosophy at the University of Berlin.

Another German of noble origin, and one who had cooperated with Willich in the Baden Revolution, was Friedrich Hecker. While studying law at a university, he came in contact with liberal ideas and embraced them with enthusiasm. He was completely taken with the liberal movement. At the outbreak of the Revolution of 1848, he joined Willich in Baden and played a prominent role there. It was he who first proclaimed the Republic. Upon the collapse of the uprising, he traveled to America to raise funds for the Revolution. When Hecker got news of the second attempt of the revolutionaries in 1849, he immediately set out for Germany. Before his arrival, however, the uprising was suppressed. Disappointed and disillusioned, Hecker returned to the farm he had purchased near Belleville, Illinois.

Belleville was a remarkable settlement in that it was composed largely of former German university students. Dr.

Hecker fitted in perfectly with these erstwhile members of the *Burschenschaften,* who now tried to till the soil. Because of their academic background and their ineptness as agriculturists they were traditionally labeled "Latin farmers." But they took an active interest in public affairs. In Belleville, which grew to fifteen thousand inhabitants, all civic offices were held by Germans. In fact, the county officers, too, were Germans. Eduard Retz was state treasurer three times, and in 1852, Gustav Körner became lieutenant governor of Illinois. In Germany Hecker and Körner had once fought a duel; now they were good friends.

Hecker and his son volunteered as privates in St. Louis and entered Sigel's Third Missouri Regiment. Later Hecker was given the command of the Eighty-second Illinois Regiment. At Chancellorsville he was shot from his saddle, but he was able to resume active service a few months later. He also participated in the Chattanooga campaign and the Battle of Missionary Ridge. On that occasion he was accused by General Hooker of having failed to carry out an order. Schurz, his superior officer, took his part and vindicated him. The quarrel was quite bitter and resulted in the transfer of Schurz and the resignation of Hecker. Having fought valiantly for three years, he was somewhat annoyed at not having been promoted. He distinguished himself, however, as a gentleman of charming personality and eloquence, rather than as a soldier.

A very colorful figure was Brigadier-General Louis Blenker. He had seen six years of service in Bavaria and had taken part in the Revolution of 1848. Like the other leading Forty-Eighters, he fled to Switzerland when the cause was lost and eventually came to the United States. In 1861, he joined the Union Army as colonel of the Eighth New York Regiment which he had raised. Largely because of his success at the first Battle of Bull Run, he was later given a brigadier's commission.

Blenker was fond of pomp and circumstance. Carl Schurz gives an amusing description of his headquarters. "His tent was unique in the elaborateness and taste of its appointments.

118

Not only officers of the army but civilians from afar came to see it, and he was lavish in his hospitality."

A number of German noblemen had come over to America to offer their services. They were attracted to Blenker's division. Attaching themselves to his staff as "additional aides-de-camp," he formed "a sort of court around him which abounded in high titles." "Blenker was often heard to give orders in this wise: 'Prince A., you will instruct Count B. to inspect the pickets tonight, and to take Baron S. with him.' But Blenker proved that a man can be a perfect stage general and at the same time a very efficient soldier. He was a thoroughly brave man, an excellent organizer, and an efficient commander. The regiment he had formed was a model regiment. . . ."

Blenker gave a brilliant reception to General McClellan in camp. In November, 1861, he organized an elaborate parade in his honor in Washington. Riding at the head with fifty-six staff officers in gaudy uniforms and seated on splendid steeds, he was followed by two thousand soldiers carrying torches and marching proudly to the music of twelve bands. Even President Lincoln was there to review the procession which was a sensation. Blenker was extremely popular, but his extravagance caused his downfall. His expenditures reached such proportions that he was obliged to retire.

One of the ablest German officers was Alexander von Schimmelpfennig. He had fought as an officer in Schleswig-Holstein and in Baden. Well-educated and level-headed, he was free of the crusading spirit which possessed so many of the Forty-Eighters. Having come to America, he settled in Philadelphia. At the outbreak of the Civil War, he joined the Union forces as colonel of the Seventy-fourth Pennsylvania, composed almost entirely of Germans. He distinguished himself at the Battle of Cross Keys and at the second Battle of Bull Run. It was there that his men drove Stonewall Jackson's troops back. As a reward for his bravery, he was named a brigadier-general.

At Chancellorsville he fought in the Eleventh Corps of Carl Schurz. As a result of poor placement, the Eleventh Corps was driven back by superior forces on a number of occasions. Generals Hook and Howard seized upon these setbacks of the Germans and tried to make them the scapegoats for their own failures. This happened at Gettysburg where Howard was in general direction of the field. Schimmelpfennig was in command of Schurz' division. The vastly superior foe drove the two divisions back in confusion down the streets of Gettysburg. At this point, Schimmelpfennig was struck by a blow from the butt of a gun and lay unconscious in the road. Upon regaining consciousness, he crawled into a cellar where he hid for two days, thus eluding capture. Later, he fought in the Carolinas where he was struck down by another foe, namely, malaria. Again he recovered sufficiently to head his troops when Charlestown surrendered.

Throughout the war Schimmelpfennig conducted himself like a gentleman and a well-trained Prussian officer. In the Baden Revolution he had been Schurz' superior officer; in the Civil War he occupied the lower rank. Both were warm friends, and Schurz, with his typical frankness, generously acknowledged that he had learned much from Schimmelpfennig.

4. "LITTLE GERMANY"

The plan of a number of German idealists to form a perfect state, a "New Germany" in America, did not meet with success. Nevertheless, because of the large concentration of Germans in many cities, communities that were typically German did develop. In the larger cities they remained minorities, but there were towns that were almost wholly German. Some of these were deliberately planned that way. A classical example is that of Egg Harbor City, New Jersey. It was an exclusively German town and remained so for over half a century. It was founded primarily as a haven for the Germans who were being molested and annoyed by members of the Knownothing movement, especially in the city of Baltimore. Their festivals were raided, and their meetings were broken up. The anti-immigrant resentment was also directed against the Irish.

On November 24, 1854, the Gloucester Town and Farm Association was organized in Philadelphia, and thirty-eight thousand acres of land in the pine woods of New Jersey were purchased. On July of the same year, the first train of a new railroad had puffed eastward through the region. The new settlement would have a railroad station. In September of 1855, the first settlers arrived.

A municipal government was organized. All meetings of the town council were conducted in German, but for the convenience of county and state officials the records were kept in English as well. Churches were built, schools were established, a newspaper was published, and dramatic and singing societies were founded. In the traditional way the streets were named to honor distinguished Germans. Toward the end of the century, however, other ethnic groups moved in, and Egg Harbor City lost its German character. Today it is still an attractive little town of cosy homes and pretty gardens, but a word of German is rarely heard.

8 · Building the Nation

The Civil War was followed by a half century of peace, progress, and prosperity. The United States made such tremendous strides that it soon outstripped the Old World in almost every field of human endeavor. With admiration, amazement, and envy Europe gazed upon the young giant flexing its muscles. There seemed to be no limit to the growth of America. As one German writer expressed it, the United States was *"das Land der unbegrenzten Möglichkeiten"*—the land of unlimited possibilities.

The significant factors, which brought about this astounding development, were: the mighty railroad systems which spanned the continent; the transformation of agriculture; the vast growth of industry; the huge waves of immigration; the expansion of world trade; and the organization of the workers.

In all of these areas the Germans played a vital part.

1. AGRICULTURE

Since the majority of German immigrants during the eighteenth and nineteenth centuries were of peasant stock, it is not surprising that they became farmers in the United States. In fact, according to the Twelfth Census of 1900, they led all other nationalities in this area, as shown in the accompanying table.

From the table on p. 123 it is seen that farmers of German parentage own 522,252 farm homes, or almost three times as many as the next largest foreign element, that of Great Britain. In fact, German farmers own almost as many farms as the next

Country	Total Private Families	Total Farm Homes	Free	Encumbered	Unknown
Germany...	1,982,917	522,252	227,266	156,253	10,054
Ireland.....	1,234,108	176,968	85,320	52,651	3,734
Great Britain...	835,513	183,157	87,786	49,278	3,987
Scandinavia	437,516	174,694	70,788	64,873	4,170
Austria-Hungary	192,068	34,870	16,261	10,629	655
Italy.......	141,635	5,321	2,091	1,005	139
Poland.....	121,971	12,478	4,795	5,725	227
Total of U.S......	14,083,882	4,906,911	2,270,194	1,042,859	111,926

* Five other groups have been omitted.

three foreign elements together, namely, Great Britain, Ireland and Scandinavia. They own over 10 per cent of all the farm homes in the United States.

Quantitatively, then, the Germans lead as farmers; qualitatively they have also distinguished themselves in a number of different types of agriculture. One of the earliest farmers to grow fruit by the acre was a German, Johann Schwerdkopf, a Hessian by birth and a gunsmith by trade. Before the Revolution he had cultivated rose bushes and herbs; about 1783, he began to raise fruits and strawberries which, in fact, soon monopolized the market.

From the earliest times German immigrants tried to raise grapes and make wine with varying success. It was an immigrant from Bremen, George Husmann, who conducted a model farm in Missouri and devoted himself particularly to viticul-

123

ture. He had taken part in the gold rush to California in 1849 and had served as a lieutenant in the Civil War before settling down as an agriculturist. In 1866, he published a book entitled *Grapes and Wine,* and three years later, he started the *Grape Culturist,* the first journal devoted to a single agricultural product. Husmann was also active in politics, as a member of the Missouri Horticultural Society and the State Board of Agriculture. He was one of the first to send cuttings of American vines to France to replenish her declining vineyards.

In 1881, he resigned his professorship at Missouri University to become the manager of the Talcoa Vineyards in Napa County, California. Believing firmly in the American grape as opposed to the European—which had deteriorated because of a pest—Husmann put viticulture on a firm basis in California. For the Paris Exposition he selected the wines which were awarded some twenty medals. Husmann's son, George C., carried on the work of his father. After managing extensive nurseries and vineyards in California, he was appointed Pomologist in Charge of Viticulture in the Bureau of Plant Industry in Washington.

German viticulturists in California did not, however, give up their dream of cultivating European grapes on American soil. The pioneer in this field was Julius Dresel, born at Geisenheim on the Rhine in 1816. After much experimentation he was finally able to drink Rhine wine produced on his own farm in Sonoma County, California. Dresel, who had studied at Heidelberg, was a Latin farmer, but a very successful one. In Texas he succeeded in raising wheat, rye, and cotton without the use of slaves. In California he experimented for many years with French and German grape vines to overcome phylloxera and to find the vines best suited to the California climate.

Germans also became interested in various types of fruit, especially the fig. They were largely instrumental in establishing orange culture, especially around the town of Anaheim, a German settlement southwest of Los Angeles.

As in most scientific areas, the Germans have been particularly strong on the theoretical side. The science of agriculture is indebted to Eugene Hilgard for its start. Born in Zweibrücken in 1833, he studied at the Universities of Freiburg, Zurich, and Heidelberg where he got his doctorate in 1853. He then occupied positions in geology, chemistry, and natural science at a number of American universities. In 1906, he published an authoritative work entitled *Soils*. His brothers were equally distinguished, one a civil engineer, the other a physician.

2. INDUSTRY

Even in early colonial days, as we have seen, the Germans established certain industries. In Jamestown they made glass; in Georgia they processed silk; in Germantown they became weavers; and in New Amsterdam they developed the fur trade. The food industries were always popular with Germans; even today, despite super markets, every American city has its German groceries and delicatessens.

Probably the most widely known name in the preserving business is that of Heinz and his fifty-seven varieties. Allegheny, Pennsylvania, became the center of the pickle industry which was controlled by two German firms, the Lutz & Schramm Company and the H. J. Heinz Company. Henry J. Heinz was born in Pittsburgh of German parentage. After starting a small food products business in Sharpsburg, he moved to Pittsburgh in 1872. The firm grew rapidly; in 1888, it assumed the name of the H. J. Heinz Company. In addition to the main plant in Pittsburgh, there are eleven branch factories, including one in Spain; sixty-seven salting stations; and twenty-six branch houses and agencies in all parts of the world. Other pickling establishments of German origin are J. O. Schimmel of Jersey City and Bosman & Lohman of Norfolk, Virginia.

That widely used breakfast cereal, oatmeal, was originated by a German, Ferdinand Schuhmacher, who was born in Hanover in 1822. He came to the United States in 1850 and became a farmer and then a grocer. In 1856, he became the original manufacturer of oatmeal in this country, putting out a popular brand known as "Rolled Oats." Also in a related field was John Hecker who originated self-rising flour.

The big name in sugar is that of Claus Spreckels who was born in Hanover in 1828. He arrived in Charleston at the age of nineteen with three dollars in his pocket. Through thrift and hard work in the grocery business he rose rapidly. In 1856, he went to California where he invested his savings in a brewery. Realizing the great opportunities in sugar, he became a workman in a sugar refining plant in New York and then returned to San Francisco to organize the Bay Sugar Refining Company.

Eager to learn more about the industry, he became a workman in a beet sugar factory in Magdeburg, Germany. He became the undisputed master of the sugar industry in time, devising new processes and improvements. He introduced the cube and the crushed sugars used today. To maintain complete control of the field, he organized the entire beet sugar industry.

In the East the sugar kings were the Havemeyers. William and Frederick Havemeyer were born in Bückeburg, Germany, where they learned sugar refining. Like Spreckels, they acquired great wealth. A grandson of William, William F. Havemeyer, was thrice elected mayor of New York.

Two Germans became prominent as stock owners in the West. These were Henry Miller, born in Württemberg, and his partner, Charles Lux, born in Baden. They owned not only the largest number of cattle, but they were also the largest landowners in California.

Another great Western cattleman was the German Jew Nelson Morris, who came to Chicago from Germany in 1856. Starting out with a job in the stockyards which paid five dollars a month, Morris invested his scant savings in pigs whose legs had been broken in transit. This local trade developed into a multimillion dollar business. Morris provided food for the Union armies during the Civil War. He was the first to send cattle on the hoof to Europe, and he also initiated the process of shipping frozen beef.

In the brewing industry the Germans have, of course, been pre-eminent. Most of the well-known names are German—Anheuser-Busch, Blatz, Schlitz, Schaefer, Ehret, and Pabst. Germans have also distinguished themselves in the hotel business. For example, George C. Boldt, president of the Waldorf-Astoria Company, was born in Germany.

In the technical branches the Germans have achieved fame in bridge construction and engineering generally. The greatest name among bridge builders is undoubtedly that of John A. Roebling, inventor of the modern suspension bridge. A graduate of the Royal Polytechnicum in Berlin, he began the manufacture of wire cables at Saxonburg near Pittsburgh. With them he constructed bridges across the Allegheny, the Monongahela, the Niagara, and the East River. In fact, the Brooklyn Bridge which spanned the East River was so great an achievement that for decades it was recognized all over the world as the symbol of New York. Unfortunately, Roebling could not see the completion of his great undertaking because of excessive physical strain incurred while directing the construction. It was his son, Washington Augustus Roebling, who finished the job.

Outstanding in the field of electrical engineering is the name of Charles P. Steinmetz, born in Breslau in 1865. He made many brilliant discoveries in the laboratories of the General Electric Company at Schenectady. As an investigator and inventor, Steinmetz is sometimes considered to be the equal of Edison.

The field of science is, of course, one favored by the Germans. In the manufacture of scientific and optical apparatus the names of Bausch & Lomb stand out. Equally distinguished in this field is Emil Meyrowitz, who was born in Danzig. Emil Berliner invented the gramophone in 1887.

In the growth of the steel industry the big name is, of course, Andrew Carnegie. His two ablest lieutenants, however, were men of German ancestry, namely, Henry C. Frick and Charles M. Schwab. In the automobile industry a German name is represented by Studebaker. The Studebakers (Staudebacher?)

are of Pennsylvania German origin, coming from the region where the Conestoga wagons were first made.

In the manufacture of musical instruments, particularly pianos, Germans have been leaders. The first pianos made in Philadelphia were by John Behrent (1775) and Charles Albrecht (1789). Well-known are the names Weber, Steck, Behning, Kranich & Bach, Sohmer, Behr, Schnabel, Krakauer, and Knabe. The greatest improvements in the instrument have been made by the Steinways.

Henry Steinway (Steinweg) was born in 1797 in Brunswick, and he learned how to build organs and pianos in Goslar. By 1825, he had established his own factory in Brunswick. Leaving his oldest son, Theodore, in charge of the factory, he emigrated to New York with his four sons. After serving an apprenticeship, he began making his own pianos, turning out one a week. Constant improvements were made, and the Steinway piano gained general favor in the concert hall. It is the acknowledged leader in that field.

Many of the German Jews, who have become department store magnates, began modestly as peddlers, trudging from door to door with their bundles on their backs. This was the case with Lazarus Straus, the founder of R. H. Macy and of Abraham & Straus, who came from Rhenish Bavaria in 1852. The Seligmans were first peddlers in the South, and Benjamin Bloomingdale, who came from Bavaria, started peddling in Kansas. In the Midwest Samuel Rosenwald began the same way.

Wealthy German Jews have distinguished themselves in the world of finance and as philanthropists. Outstanding among them are Otto H. Kahn, who supported the Metropolitan Opera; Bache and Altman, who gave their magnificent art collections to the Metropolitan Museum of Art; Solomon Guggenheim, who supported three foundations; Jacob H. Schiff and his son-in-law, Felix M. Warburg, who gave huge sums to libraries and various philanthropies; and Julius Rosenwald, who gave more than $30,000,000 to be spent for the benefit of mankind. Of this sum, $22,000,000 were to be spent on

128

Negroes. One of the beneficiaries of this money was the singer, Marion Anderson.

3. LABOR RELATIONS

During the nineteenth century the Socialist movement, which was deeply concerned with the labor movement in the United States was almost entirely under the dominance of the Germans. Its founder was Wilhelm Weitling, who was born in Magdeburg in 1808 and came to America in 1846. As a journeyman tailor, he had the opportunity to travel widely in Europe and was well-known among the workmen's circles in Zurich, Paris, Brussels, and London. He was an effective speaker and writer and a man of winning personality.

He had come to the States at the invitation of a group of Free-Soilers to take charge of the publication of their journal. At the outbreak of the Revolution of 1848, he returned to Germany. After the collapse of the revolt, he came to New York where he became active in the labor movement. He advocated many social reforms.

In 1850, the Central Committee of United Trades was organized, and a weekly, *Republik der Arbeiter,* was founded. The mass meetings and the volume of publications put out by the *Republik* attracted the attention of workmen of other ethnic groups. From October 22 to 28, 1851, the German working groups held their first national convention in Philadelphia. Ten of the largest cities of the country were represented. Weitling, who was the leader, became so dictatorial, however, that he was forced to withdraw not only from the convention, but from public life in general. He spent the rest of his days as a clerk in the Bureau of Immigration.

The *Allgemeine Arbeiterbund* declined, too, until Joseph Wedemeyer, a personal friend of Marx and Engels, came over and took charge. He lectured in German and English in an attempt to spread the theories of Karl Marx. In 1858, the League again declined because of its selection of Gustav Struve, a visionary revolutionist, as the editor of its weekly, *Soziale Republik.*

Socialist ideas also spread to the *Turnvereine,* which were primarily athletic clubs, but which from the start had combined ideals of political freedom with their gymnastics. *Turnerei,* or gymnastics, had been founded in the *Hasenheide* near Berlin in 1811 by the sturdy patriot, Friedrich Ludwig Jahn. His ideal was vigorous and independent manhood, sound in body and in mind. The movement spread rapidly throughout Germany. It was halted in 1819 by reactionary elements who feared its message of freedom, and Jahn was thrown into prison.

Enthusiastic disciples of Jahn spread the movement to other countries. It was brought to America as early as 1824 by Carl Beck and Carl Follen. They were active in setting up a gymnasium in the Round Hill School in Northampton, Massachusetts. Francis Lieber, who arrived in 1827, had the first swimming pool built in Boston. German-American gymnastic clubs were organized all over, and by 1859 there were 152 *Turnvereine* with a membership of over 3000. In 1850, the Turners formed a national body, the *Vereinigte Turnvereine Nordamerikas,* the name of which was changed the following year to *Sozialistischer Turnerbund.*

In 1857, a communist club was organized in New York which arranged an elaborate commemorative festival on the tenth anniversary of the Revolution of 1848. That such radical organizations could be founded and allowed to conduct meetings unmolested, is a great compliment to the democratic and broad-minded spirit prevailing in the United States at that time. There were, of course, many native Americans, who became alarmed at the pronouncement of radical reformers and labor leaders and suspicious of foreigners in general, particularly Germans.

It must be stressed, however, that the rank and file of these German-American organizations were thrifty, honest, and hardworking citizens and that the leaders were noble and frequently visionary idealists. The test of their loyalty came when the Civil War broke out. Since the abolition of slavery had always been a basic tenet of the German-Americans, the great majority supported the Union cause with enthusiasm. However the Turners were especially active. Most of the *Vereine* sent more than half their membership; in New York, an entire regiment was organized within a few days. In Missouri, several regiments consisted almost completely of Turners. Joseph Weydemeyer, August Willich, and Fritz Jacobi who had been leaders in communist clubs distinguished themselves on the battlefield. In fact, the war absorbed the energies of the socialists so much that the movement was dormant until after 1867.

In 1864, under the leadership of Marx, Engels, and Mazzini, the First International was organized in London. Four years later sections were established in New York, Chicago, and San Francisco. Most of the original members were Germans, but later on native Americans and representatives of other ethnic groups joined. Several energetic Forty-Eighters, like F. A. Sorge and Dr. Adolph Douai, assumed the leadership of the American International. A Labor Reform Party was organized and Douai became one of the leading exponents of socialism in the United States through his editorship of the *New Yorker Volkszeitung* from 1878 to 1888.

In 1877, the Socialist Labor Party of North America was founded in Newark, New Jersey. For twenty years it dominated the socialist movement in the United States. Its membership was generally foreign, chiefly German.

During the last quarter of the nineteenth century an even more violent streak of lightning flashed upon the American scene. In 1882, a passionate radical named John Most went from city to city preaching anarchism. Born in Augsburg in 1846, he had led an unhappy and tempestuous life. His home life with a cruel stepmother and labor under a tyrannical employer had embittered him toward society. Because of his radical activities, he was thrown into prison in Austria, Saxony, and Prussia. For congratulating the Nihilists on assassinating Alexander II, he was sentenced in London to sixteen months of hard labor. Surprisingly enough, Most had considerable success in the United States, and in 1883, a convention of anarchists at Pittsburgh proclaimed "communistic anarchism." A central group was formed in Chicago where disaster struck the movement. Because of police interference at a labor meeting, a protest gathering was held in the Haymarket. Unfortunately, though, a bomb was thrown as the police were dispersing the crowd. Indiscriminate firing began, and after the fray was over, seven police and four workingmen lay dead with a hundred persons wounded.

The anarchists were held entirely responsible for the affair. Of the ten leaders indicted, six were Germans, and they were prosecuted for murder. The judgment of the lower court was upheld by the Supreme Court. Four of the prisoners were hanged in 1887, and three were given life sentences. In 1893, Governor Altgeld granted absolute pardons to these three, with the comment that "the judge was biased, the jury packed, the defendants not proven guilty, the trial illegal."

This courageous action of Governor Altgeld infuriated large sections of the population and provoked a hysterical outburst of abuse. He was denounced as a scoundrel, a traitor, and an anarchist. Actually, as Harry Barnard makes clear in his biography, *Eagle Forgotten*, Peter Altgeld was "a very archetype of Americanism, believing in justice, decency, calmness, order, progress."

John Peter Altgeld, born in Nassau, Germany, in 1847, was brought by his parents to America, and they settled near Mansfield, Ohio. At the age of sixteen he entered the Union Army and fought until the end of the war. He had to struggle to get enough of an education to enable him to become a schoolteacher. At the age of twenty-one he left his father's farm, tramping as far as Kansas, and then went back to Missouri. Shoeless, in rags, starving, and racked by fever, he found shelter and kindness in the little village of Savannah. There he became a lawyer, demonstrating remarkable mental acumen from the start. Less than a year after becoming prosecuting attorney of Andrew County, he opened an office in Chicago and married a childhood sweetheart. The "little Dutchman," once the ragged tramp, had made good. Within a few years he was a millionaire as a result of shrewd speculation in land.

132

A brilliant orator, he was quickly attracted to politics, and in 1886, he was elected to the Superior Court of Cook County. At this time the seething labor conditions in Chicago came to a climax. Many brutalities and injustices had been perpetrated on the laboring classes, and they listened eagerly to the lurid message of the anarchists. Of course, their cries reeked of the inferno to the wealthy citizens, who sought the ruthless extirpation of the radicals. This, the police tried to carry out. On the other hand, there is no remaining doubt that all the men convicted for the Haymarket bombing were innocent. Altgeld proved this irrefutably in an eighteen thousand word document.

Altgeld had been elected to the governorship of Illinois in 1893, the first governor of foreign birth. During the first year of his administration the World's Columbia Exposition was held in Chicago. The next year a strike occurred in the Pullman Works. When President Cleveland sent federal troops to quell the strike, Altgeld rebuked him. Later, he was the principal factor in the victory of the bimetallists at the Democratic convention of 1896. But for his German birth, Altgeld, not Bryan, would have been the nominee.

His most daring act, however, was the pardoning of the anarchists, Fielden, Neebe, and Schwab. He became deeply interested in penal problems and succeeded in introducing a new spirit into the prisons and reformatories of the state. His book, *Our Penal Machinery and Its Victims* became a classic. Many of the constructive social measures that he advocated were later incorporated into the law. When Altgeld died in 1902, tens of thousands of admirers filed reverently past the bier of the courageous man.

4. IMMIGRATION

German immigration in the eighteenth century had been numbered in hundreds of thousands; in the nineteenth century it went into the millions. In fact, it reached a total larger than that of any other nationality, as is seen in the accompanying tabulation.

Germany	5,009,280
Ireland	3,871,253
Great Britain	3,024,222
Scandinavia	1,439,060
Canada	1,049,939
Italy	1,040,457
Austria-Hungary	1,027,195
Russia & Poland	926,902
All other	1,726,913
Total	**19,115,221**

The German immigration, by decades, as given in the census reports, is as follows:

1821–1830	6,761
1831–1840	152,454
1841–1850	434,626
1851–1860	951,667
1861–1870	787,468
1871–1880	718,182
1881–1890	1,452,970
1891–1900	505,152
	5,009,280

Until 1850, the German immigration was exceeded by the Irish. From 1851 to 1860, however, the German immigration outnumbered the Irish and all others. It continued to do so until the last decade of the nineteenth century, when it fell below the Slavic and Italian immigrations.

The causes for immigration during the nineteenth century were overpopulation, destructive wars, the ruin of small industries through the factories, and the failure to achieve political freedom in Germany. The waves of immigration varied in accordance with periods of depression on the Continent and periods of prosperity in the United States.

The crest of the wave from 1850 to 1854 coincided with the Revolution of 1848 in Germany. Poor economic conditions and failure of crops caused later migrations. The improvements in ocean travel, the opening of the West by the railroads, and the efforts made by midwestern states to attract settlers, stimulated emigration from Germany. Thus, immigration increased after the Civil War. The desire to escape military service impelled many Germans to emigrate after the Franco-Prussian War. It was one of the chief reasons for leaving the Reich.

A great upsurge came in 1880, when immigration was three times as large as in 1879. In 1881, it almost reached 250,000. The banner year, though, was 1882 with 250,630, a record which has never been surpassed. Large numbers of Germans came until 1885; after 1892 the numbers declined, due to Germany's expansion in industry and material prosperity.

The total immigration for all countries continued to rise, until it went beyond a million in the years 1905, 1906, and 1907. After slight declines it again went beyond a million in 1910, 1913, and 1914. Then a decline set in which reached a low of 28,781 in 1942.

The ethnic composition of the immigration changed after 1880. Up to that time, three-fourths of all the immigrants had come from northern and western Europe; from that decade on immigrants from southern and eastern Europe predominated. In the decade of the eighties, Italian, Austrian, and Polish immigrants made up 19 per cent of the total. In the decade of the nineties, they made up 49 per cent of the total, and in the first decade of the twentieth century, they constituted 66 per cent of the total.

The attitude toward immigrants had changed, too. Whereas formerly they had been invited, yea, enticed to come to our shores, various steps were now taken to keep them out. The restriction of immigration began before the turn of the century.

There were a number of reasons for this critical attitude toward the newcomer. The leaders in the radical movements, which began around 1848—socialism, communism, anarchism— had all been foreigners. The Chicago Haymarket Riot of 1886 focused attention on this situation, for only one of the ten leaders indicted was a native American. As early as 1887

Chauncey M. Depew called for the restriction of immigration to keep out undesirable radicals.

American labor groups were also hostile to a free influx of immigrants, who, they maintained, were brought in as cheap labor to depress wages and break strikes. Finally, the slums and the increase in crime were blamed on the immigrants.

The first immigrants to be restricted, in fact, excluded, were the Chinese, by an act passed in 1882. Then various laws followed: prohibition of laborers under contract, imposition of a head tax, literacy test, etc. The extreme was reached in 1957 when quotas were established for various nationalities. These were very small, compared to the immigration figures of the latter part of the nineteenth century. For the Irish it was 17,756; for the Germans, 25,814. The total for all nationalities is only 154,857.

From the eighties onward, immigration from southern and eastern Europe predominated. However, from 1932, another entirely different type of immigrant reached our shores, due to happenings on the Continent. That was the German Jew. In general, he did not belong to the working class; he was usually well-educated, professionally trained, and conservative in his views.

German immigration, then, falls into the following categories: the first period, during which German laborers, tradesmen, and peasants went to the states of the eastern coast and to the Midwest to become farmers and businessmen; the second period, around 1848, when large numbers came over because of the political oppression in Europe and went into the cities to become journalists, white-collar workers, and businessmen, rather than farmers; the third period, after 1866, which was again a working class movement with better educated workers, however, than at the beginning of the century; and finally the arrival of the refugees in the thirties.

5. CULTURAL CONTRIBUTIONS

Although the majority of the Germans that have come to the United States belong to the working class, there have been many among them who were intellectually gifted and who made significant contributions to the cultural life of our country. Some of these have already been described in connection with the conditions in the various colonies and the settling of the new states.

Even in the earliest times and in the smallest settlements, attempts were made to establish churches and schools. The settlers had behind them a tradition of good schools. Protestants as well as Catholics established parochial schools in which German was usually the medium of instruction. In many communities the German schools were superior to the public schools and thereby raised educational standards.

At the beginning of the nineteenth century, German scholars like Carl Beck and Carl Follen exerted a deep influence on the schools of Boston. In fact, they were the ones who introduced physical training into the curriculum. The kindergarten, too, was a German contribution.

The deepest influences, however, did not come through German-Americans, but rather through American educators whose attention was drawn to the excellence of the schools of Germany. The greatest influence in this connection was the report in 1837 of Victor Cousin, a French official, who had visited German schools. His laudatory report, which was translated into English, did more than anything else to introduce German educational ideas in this country.

One of the ideals of those who favored the establishment of private schools, was the preservation of German language and culture. As a result of social and economic pressures, there was always the danger that the younger generation would drop the use of German. Since the German schools maintained such high standards, the public schools did not offer much competition. A special training seminary for teachers was established in Milwaukee to supply well-trained teachers.

It is interesting to note at this point that among the strongest advocates of the maintenance of German were the German Jews. They insisted on the German language for their children, even in such Yankee communities as Bangor, Maine. One of

137

the most ardent champions of German culture was the Reform Rabbi David Einhorn, who came to America in 1855. He said to his congregation, "Is not the German spirit the bearer of Reform Judaism?"

Jewish children were exposed to German lessons, German sermons, and German prayers. The battle between English and German grew more pronounced during the 1860's and 70's, and it was not till then that congregations decided to keep their records in English instead of German.

A truly significant contribution in the field of modern language instruction was made by Maximilian Berlitz, born in Württemberg in 1852. He came to the United States in 1869, like many an immigrant, with great hope and very little money. He worked first as a watchmaker, and it was not until 1878 that he opened a language school to introduce his new method. His success followed almost immediately, and he soon began establishing schools in large cities throughout the country. In fact, he founded over four hundred schools throughout the world, and the name Berlitz is now known from Maine to Madagascar. In recognition of his services, Berlitz was honored by various governments. France made him a chevalier, and the Sultan of Morocco bestowed knighthood upon him.

With the increase in immigration and the settlement of large numbers of Germans in town, a greater interest in good music arose. The earliest musical society in New England was formed as a result of William Billings' music class in 1774. However, the most influential of the New England choral societies was the Handel and Haydn Society, founded in Boston in 1815.

Boston may also claim the honor of having had the first organ-builder in America, Eduard Bromfield, who constructed his first instrument in 1745. The first American piano, however, was built in Philadelphia by John Behrent.

One of the prime movers in the Handel and Haydn Society was a German, Gottlieb Graupner, in whose music shop at 6 Franklin Street the first session was held. In 1854, a professional conductor, Carl Zerrahn from Mecklenburg, was appointed. He served the Society for more than forty years.

138

Graupner, himself, was more than a music shop owner; he may be called the father of American orchestral music. He had been an oboist in a Hanoverian regiment before coming to London, where he played the same instrument in a large orchestra. Shortly after arriving in Boston, he gathered a group of professionals and amateurs about him for practice, and in 1810, he formed the Philharmonic Society. Its ten or twelve players used to meet on Saturday evenings to play Haydn symphonies and other works from the classical repertoire. Gradually it grew in size and fame.

In Philadelphia an orchestra was started even earlier. By 1783, a group of musicians from Hamburg had formed a band. A more pretentious and influential organization, however, was the Musical Fund Society founded in 1820. It arranged sacred and secular programs, gave instrumental and vocal concerts, constructed a music hall, and assisted indigent musicians. It continued to give concerts until 1857.

In the second quarter of the nineteenth century New York took the lead in orchestral music. The Philharmonic Society was founded by Uriah G. Hill, who had studied in Germany with Louis Spohr. He was assisted by a German named Henry C. Timm. Born in Hamburg in 1811, he remained president of the society for many years. The society gave its first concert in December, 1842, with an orchestra of sixty pieces. All of its great leaders were Germans: Theodore Eisfeld, Carl Bergmann, Leopold Damrosch, Theodore Thomas, Adolph Neuendorff, Anton Seidl, Walter Damrosch, and Emil Paur. In fact, twenty-two of the fifty-two musicians were Germans; in 1865, some seventy out of eighty-one were Germans; by 1895 in an orchestra of ninety-four all but five were Germans.

Outstanding among the conductors of the Philharmonic was Theodore Thomas. Born in Esens, Hanover, in 1835, he came to America at the age of ten. Despite the fact that there was a Philharmonic Society already, Thomas began a series of symphonic *soirées* in 1864. These were discontinued when in 1879 he was called to the directorship of the Cincinnati College of Music. However, two years later he returned to New York to

139

become the conductor of the New York Philharmonic. He introduced what were then the newer and younger composers like Wagner, Liszt, Berlioz, Brahms, and Saint-Saens.

Due to his influence orchestras were founded in many other large cities. In fact, Thomas himself helped to develop the musical taste of the Midwest. In 1869, he gave three concerts in Chicago, and from 1879 to 1881, he was the director of the Musical College of Cincinnati. As a conductor, Thomas distinguished himself by his leadership and his interpretation. There were soon orchestras in the cities of Philadelphia, Baltimore, Pittsburgh, Cincinnati, Washington, Buffalo, St. Louis, Indianapolis, Cleveland, and San Francisco. For a long time these orchestras were generally conducted by Germans or Americans of German descent or training.

6. PRIDE IN PRUSSIAN PROWESS

Although German-Americans during the last quarter of the nineteenth century were primarily occupied with domestic issues, such as sound money and local option, certain events in Germany did absorb their interest and emotions. In 1848, they had been stirred by the revolutionary upheavals on the Continent, and in 1870, the Franco-Prussian War engaged their attention.

Their sentiment, as reflected in the German press, was practically unanimous in support of the home country. This was not true, however, of their attitude toward the various political developments leading up to the conflict. The liberals of 1830 and the radicals of 1848 had been enthusiastically for German unification, but when censorship, repression, and the stifling of democratic aspirations were used as means to achieve that unification, the German-American press became sharply critical. They viewed the rise of Prussia and its development into a military state with some misgivings. Bismarck's policies were condemned, and the war between Prussia and Austria in 1866 evoked little enthusiasm. There was also some difference of opinion between North Germans and South Germans, Prussians and Bavarians.

140

Nothing, however, succeeds like success and, when the Germans gained one victory after another and then captured Paris, the doubters were easily won over. The newspapers reported these victories with exciting headlines. Their readers read the reports with bated breath. After many centuries of disunity and impotence, at last the German states would be welded into a powerful, unified nation. Germany would be one of the major powers of Europe.

The startling events and the military successes did more than anything else to unite the Germans in the United States. Even the Forty-Eighters and the liberals were won over, hoping that Germany would become more democratic after its unification.

Not all, however, joined in the general outburst of jubilation; a few lone voices were raised in the wilderness. The intransigeant Karl Heinzen, who had participated in the Revolution of 1848, and who had written vitriolic diatribes against the Prussian bureaucracy for years, was one of the most outspoken dissenters. In his *Pionier* he expressed extreme hostility toward the new Germany, which he said was dominated by the Junkers, the police and the military. Several German papers in New York and Philadelphia objected to the glorification of the Iron Chancellor. In fact, one New York paper, the *Arbeiter Union,* preferred to go into bankruptcy, rather than change its anti-war point of view. A number of German workmen's associations protested against the war with France. Carl Schurz, then Senator Schurz, accused the secretary of war under Grant of sending surplus war materials to Europe and, in doing so, forced a congressional investigation.

The unification of Germany made the greatest impact on the German-American element in the United States during the nineteenth century. There was not only unrestrained joy that the Fatherland had been united, but there was the feeling that the status of the German would be greatly improved abroad. They hoped that the prejudices and hostilities directed toward them would be overcome. Thus, the public displays of elation knew no bounds. There were parades and huge mass meetings in New York, Chicago, Cleveland, and St. Louis. The

141

jubilation expressed itself in oratory and song, drinking and dancing. Large sums were collected to be sent to the widows and orphans of the soldiers who had lost their lives in the conflict.

The "Grays" and the "Greens," stirred by romantic and idealistic notions, had in past years engaged in crusades for improving government and ameliorating social conditions in the States. Their radical tendencies gradually subsided, and they became more conservative. The average German-American was more concerned with improving his economic condition and enjoying himself in his *Verein,* than with political issues. He was an industrious, thrifty, honest citizen, without the slightest desire to fight for any social ideals.

This attitude was reflected in the German press which took an upswing because of the establishment of the German Empire. New arrivals from Germany, who had trained as journalists, were hired. They were, in the main, completely ignorant of the issues that had stirred Americans during the middle of the nineteenth century. Furthermore, they were not political radicals; they believed in the recently unified Germany and its rulers. Greater stress was given European, especially German, news.

On the other hand, the German press tended to become more American. It was, after all, dependent upon American business and American advertising for its support, and this conditioned its attitude toward domestic issues. The days of Karl Heinzen were gone. No longer did an editor dare to express radical, personal views or proclaim revolutionary ideals. Publishing a newspaper was primarily a commercial enterprise, and foreign language editors were obliged to imitate the methods of their English language colleagues.

9 ⁄ War and Peace

1. THE STILLNESS BEFORE THE STORM

At the turn of the century, the relations between the United States and Germany were warm and cordial. When Theodore Roosevelt visited Emperor William in Berlin after his hunting trip in Africa, the two got along famously. William II, later denounced as the war mongering kaiser, was acclaimed as one of the best guarantees for peace in Europe. As a result, the German sovereign inaugurated an exchange of professors with America in 1902. The American chair at the University of Berlin, endowed by James Speyer, was named the Theodore Roosevelt Professorship. In 1904, Professor Münsterberg of Harvard—then one of the leading psychologists—published his two volumes entitled *Die Amerikaner*. This sympathetic treatment of the United States contributed greatly to a more intimate understanding between the two countries.

Andrew D. White, who twice represented the United States in Germany, praised the Germans for their idealism and their "higher and better development of man. . . ." "In no land," said he, "has this idea penetrated more deeply than in Germany, and it is this idea which should penetrate more and more American thought and practice." And, when Prince Henry of Prussia, the emperor's brother, visited the United States in 1902, he was welcomed everywhere with parades and banquets.

Most German-language newspapers devoted more space to domestic issues such as prohibition and women's suffrage than to the political situation in Europe. Occasionally, some anti-

143

British sentiment would appear. Now and then, concern was expressed over ethnic frictions within Austria-Hungary or the sinister designs of Russia. Nor did the German emperor's outbursts about *die gelbe Gefahr* or the *Drang nach Osten* cause much of a stir. On the whole, sweetness and light prevailed.

2. THE TEMPEST BREAKS

Suddenly, during the warm days of July, 1914, like a bolt of lightning from a cloudless sky, war broke out in Europe. At first the reactions of most German-Americans did not differ from those of their fellow citizens of other ethnic backgrounds. They were surprised, startled, and shocked.

It is of interest to note the numbers of the principal European elements in the United States at the outbreak of the First World War. The total population of the country at that time was 91,972,266 (census of 1910).

Country of Origin	Foreign Born	Both Parents Foreign-Born	One Parent Foreign-Born	Totals
Germany..........	2,501,181	3,911,847	1,869,590	8,282,618
Ireland............	1,352,155	2,141,577	1,010,628	4,504,360
England, Scotland, Wales...........	1,219,968	852,610	1,158,474	3,231,052
Russia, Finland......	1,732,421	949,316	70,938	2,752,675
Austria-Hungary.....	1,670,524	900,129	131,133	2,701,786
Italy..............	1,343,070	695,187	60,103	2,098,360
Total all countries, including those not listed.......	13,345,545	12,916,311	5,981,526	32,243,382

Americans as a whole hoped that the conflict would remain a local struggle—a quarrel to be settled between Austria and Serbia. The assassination of the Archduke Francis Ferdinand

144

at Serajevo, June 28, 1914, did not cause too much excitement. However, when it became evident that a general European conflagration was developing, most people felt that it behooved the United States to adhere to its historic policy of neutrality. George Washington and his principle of avoiding entangling alliances was frequently quoted. In fact, America felt quite secure. The practically unanimous attitude of the press was summarized by the Literary Digest in the words: "Our isolated position and freedom from entangling alliances inspire our press with the cheering assurance that we are in no peril of being drawn into the European quarrel."

The German press in the beginning expressed views which did not differ sharply with those of other American papers. However, as one nation after another was drawn into the conflict, sides were taken. Americans could not easily forget the land of their birth and their cultural heritage. Feeling soon became bitter between pro-Ally and pro-German sympathizers, and this was reflected in the newspapers. As George Bernard Shaw said, "America, to judge by some of its papers, is mad with British patriotism, Polish nationality, and Belgian freedom."

German newspapers and magazines denounced "perfidious Albion" and published the official German versions of the causes of the conflict. The Fatherland was reluctantly obliged to resort to arms, since it was threatened by Russian Pan-Slavism and by British envy of its phenomenal growth in industry and expansion of world trade. France sought revenge for its ignominious defeat in 1870. Germany, *sans peur et sans reproche*, was arming to defend its homeland against these unconscionable enemies. Since the German war machine was a highly efficient one, the aggressors would be speedily eliminated.

It was evident that the American public was dividing into two camps. The melting pot had not melted, or amalgamated, as effectively as had been thought. President Wilson called for neutrality in thought as well as in deed. This was a noble ideal, but hardly workable. Human beings are, for the greater

145

part, guided by emotion rather than reason, especially in times of stress. As one editor put it, only persons mentally paralyzed could be neutral in thought. Furthermore, President Wilson himself did not remain neutral. He angered German-Americans by his obvious English sympathies. When, in December, 1915, the United States minister to Belgium remarked to Wilson, "I ought to tell you that in my heart there is no such thing as neutrality; I am heart and soul for the Allies," Wilson replied, "So am I. No decent man, knowing the situation and Germany, could be anything else."

Walter Hines Page, the American ambassador at the Court of St. James, was entirely pro-British. So were Wilson's two most trusted advisers, Colonel House and Robert Lansing. The only member of the Cabinet who did not have pro-British leanings was William Jennings Bryan.

Realizing the importance of having the United States on their side, the belligerents did everything in their power to gain American sympathy. Propaganda missions were organized, and much material was printed. The German government sent over Dr. Heinrich Albert and Dr. Bernhard Dernburg, and an information bureau was opened on Broadway in New York. This office sent out materials and press releases and arranged for interviews, lectures, and the showing of motion pictures. The lecturers addressed not only German language groups, but anti-war, pacifist, and Irish organizations. The *New York Daily Mail* was bought and support was given to *The Fatherland,* a weekly edited by George Sylvester Viereck.

The German language newspapers were wholly on the German side. The charge that they were bought by German money has not been substantiated. In fact, it would have been unnecessary: their strong emotional response was a natural and a sincere one. It was a question of defending the institutions and the culture of one's ancestors.

Maintaining the traditional American ideals of freedom of the press and freedom of expression, officials did not interfere. The German language press was permitted to praise the Germans and denounce their enemies. German-American organizations were not hampered in their efforts to raise funds for the support of German widows and orphans. Central offices were set up where little Iron Crosses were distributed to those who made donations of gold and jewelry.

A number of the German language newspapers attempted to reach the English speaking public by publishing material in English. As early as 1914, the *New Yorker Staats-Zeitung*—which carried at its masthead the statement, "An American Newspaper Printed in German"—began publishing a section in English entitled "The War Situation from Day to Day." German language papers in other cities did the same thing. Articles, written by German consuls, were published, and prominent Americans, favorably disposed toward Germany, were quoted.

Daily editorials were published to prove the righteousness of the German cause and to refute the attacks on the Kaiser as an autocrat. The resentment toward the American press grew daily, particularly because of its enthusiastic support of the British point of view. The inflammatory headlines rapidly built up a war psychology. German-American leaders became alarmed. They organized protest meetings and censured American editors for their one-sided handling of the news. On the other hand, the German language dailies exultantly proclaimed every new victory of the German forces. Very few voiced even the slightest criticism of the actions of the Central Powers.

The severest blow to German prestige in the United States was the invasion of Belgium and the reference to the treaty as "a scrap of paper." The British report of the alleged atrocities committed by German soldiers undoubtedly did more than anything else to inflame the emotions of hostile Americans. The German language press rejected the atrocity stories as British propaganda, but the hateful term "Hun" was applied to all Germans.

3. SWEPT INTO THE HOLOCAUST

Until the very last moment German-American leaders strained every nerve to prevent America's entrance into the war. A wave of patriotic feeling swept the numerous German-American societies. Countless affairs were arranged to raise funds to help the German cause. In New York, where the largest concentration of Americans of German descent lived, huge bazaars were held in the old Madison Square Garden. These were highly successful; the one in 1916 netted over $700,000.

American feeling, however, continued to become increasingly anti-German. The ruthless invasion of Belgium was made worse by the German chancellor's cynical comment that the neutrality treaty had been but a "scrap of paper." American sympathy was aroused for "poor little Belgium" and its heroic resistance. The climax was capped with the sinking of the *Lusitania* on May 7, 1915. The loss of 1198 passengers in 18 minutes, among them 128 United States citizens brought the war close to the American people.

British propaganda used these devastating facts with telling effect; they did not even have to be embellished. Working in a quiet and discreet manner, the British were able to exert a deep influence on American thinking. One great advantage over German propaganda was the use of a common language. The other was the strict censorship of all cables to the United States. "Three-fourths of the dispatches written by American correspondents in Central Europe perished under the shears of the British censors." After a while, those who read English newspapers in the United States got only British versions of the happenings in Europe. English catch-phrases like "the Kaiser, the Beast of Berlin," "the vicious Huns," and "the war to make the world safe for democracy" were generally adopted.

Slowly but steadily, America became involved in the war, at first only emotionally, then economically. Enormous quantities of munitions were shipped to the Allies. In August, 1916, a $500,000,000 Anglo-French loan was floated. A total of 1,567 individuals and brokerage houses subscribed to this loan. When the United States entered the war, $2,300,000,000 had been loaned to the Allies. Germany, which had also made efforts to borrow money, got only $27,000,000.

The inability of the Central Powers to present their case fairly and the incessant denunciation of everything German, caused many Americans of German ancestry to become more pro-German than they would have been otherwise. They were outraged by having the epithet "Hun" applied to their relatives here and abroad; they were incensed both with Wilson's attacks on "hyphenated Americans" and his questioning of their loyalty.

The hyphen caused a great deal of excitement. Strictly speaking, it is merely a typographical symbol linking two nouns, the first of which assumes an adjectival function. It comes from the Greek *hypo* meaning "under" and *hen* meaning "one." German-American, Italo-American, Irish-American are descriptive terms without any disparaging connotation. Wilson's indiscretion in the use of "hyphen" in reference to German-Americans evoked their deep-seated hatred for him.

Wilson, however, was mild and gentlemanly compared with the ebullient Theodore Roosevelt. The great Rough Rider, who had once been the favorite of German-American editors, now became their most rabid enemy. They said they would rather vote for Wilson than for Roosevelt, given no other choice. The wielder of the big stick was unrestrained in his vilification of the German-Americans and in his denunciation of Wilson. He lashed away at "Professor Wilson," "that Byzantine logothete," supported by "flubdubs, mollycoddles, and flapdoodle pacifists." His ranting speeches antagonized the more sensible leaders in the Republican Party, so that they did not choose him, but rather the dignified, calm Charles Evans Hughes for their presidential candidate in the election of 1916.

Although Hughes said he was for "undiluted Americanism," he did not bring up the issue of hyphenism during the campaign. His nomination did not at first arouse great enthusiasm among German-Americans, but they were greatly relieved that Roosevelt had not been chosen as the standard bearer. They accepted Hughes and gave him their support. During the campaign the editors of German language papers stressed Wilson's pro-British sympathies and campaigned against the attempts to Anglicize America. They emphasized the idea that, although foreign-born minorities were willing to be Americanized, there was a great difference between becoming an "American" and an "Anglo-Saxon."

On election night when the first returns came in, it appeared as if Hughes had won by a landslide. The voters, however, in the Midwest and Far West, who were strongly against involvement in the war, turned the tide for Wilson who won by the narrowest of margins. His slogan, "He kept us out of war," proved its effectiveness.

Both parties had tried to win the votes of the minorities. Actually, the German-Americans influenced the outcome very little. Wilson carried such notably German cities as Milwaukee and St. Louis. Probably not a single electoral vote was determined by the German-Americans.

In Europe, meanwhile, the Germans had been triumphant in the East, but were stopped on the western front. A peace offensive was launched, which was acclaimed by the German language press. President Wilson seemed ready to negotiate, and he was applauded as an honest friend of peace. Of course, there were some who were suspicious of his "peace without victory" speech. The peace offensive failed, and tension between America and Germany increased.

The apologists for Germany had an increasingly difficult time. All sorts of acts of espionage and intrigue were uncovered. Dr. Dumba, the Austrian ambassador, and Captain von Papen and Boy-Ed, German military attachés in Washington, were implicated in plots to cause sabotage in munitions factories. The German intrigues were handled with astounding clumsiness.

At one point, too, the British committed a serious blunder. In July, 1916, the British government issued a blacklist of 85

American firms that were suspected of dealing with the enemy; consequently, English concerns were forbidden to trade with them. This caused quite a stir. Even the *New York Times* called the action "tactless, foolish, and unnecessary . . ."

Events moved swiftly. In February, 1917, the German government announced its resumption of unrestricted submarine warfare. In March, large headlines shocked the nation by the revelation that German Foreign Secretary Zimmermann had cabled the German minister in Mexico, ordering him to arrange a military alliance with Mexico. As an inducement, the recovery of the "lost provinces" of Texas, New Mexico, and Arizona was held out in return for a possible Mexican declaration of war against the United States. A wave of resentment and anger swept over the nation.

It was evident that America was moving toward war. Frantic efforts were made by the German-American press and by peace societies to prevent the final step. On April 2, 1917, President Wilson asked Congress to recognize the fact that Germany was waging war on the United States. Two days later the Senate passed the war resolution by a vote of 82 to 6. The House approved by a vote of 373 to 50.

On April 6, 1917, the United States entered the First World War.

4. RESPITE

The war was over at the end of 1918, although the resolution establishing peace with Germany was not signed until July 2, 1921. German-Americans heaved a great sigh of relief. The hostility toward everything German, which had been rampant during the war, gradually subsided.

The German language was no longer banned. The enrollments in the public high schools and in the colleges grew with amazing rapidity. In New York City where only forty students of German in one high school had remained, the registers in German were above twenty thousand within a few years. Wagner operas were again given at the Metropolitan Opera House, and liberty cabbage and *sauerbraten* resumed their good old Teutonic names. The editors of German language papers breathed more freely. They began to write again with fear and restraint, pointing with pride to the contributions of German-Americans in men and money during the war. They also felt free to voice criticism again, especially toward policies detrimental to the weak and struggling Weimar Republic.

Conditions in Germany were depressing. The country was staggering beneath the colossal and fantastic reparations load of thirty-three billion dollars which the Allied powers had imposed in 1921. By 1923, German economy had broken down. Six million were out of work, and a large portion of the population was starving. Emigration from Germany had practically ceased, for the Allies had seized all the ships and had curtailed German sea operations. A mere trickle of immigrants entered the United States. When, in 1927, a German ship again entered New York harbor for the first time, German-American societies made it a gala occasion.

Things in Germany looked a little brighter, too. In 1924, the reparations payments were considerably eased by the adoption of the Dawes Plan. Two years later Germany was admitted to the League of Nations. Several international events, in which persons of German blood distinguished themselves, helped to raise the morale of the German-Americans. One of these was the swimming of the English Channel on August 6, 1926, by Gertrude Ederle. She covered the twenty-one miles in fourteen hours and thirty-one minutes, thereby breaking previous records. Her father was born in Württemberg, and her mother came from East Prussia.

In 1928, two great triumphs in aviation were achieved by Germans. In April, Baron G. von Hünefeld, together with Captains Kohl and Fitz-Maurice and a crew of six, flew from Dublin to Labrador. The reception they got in New York equalled that given to Lindbergh the previous year after his flight from the United States to Paris. In the fall of the same year, Hugo Eckner flew his huge dirigible from Friedrichshafen on Lake Constance to Lakehurst, New Jersey—a momentous event. The big ship carried twenty passengers and a crew of thirty-eight.

Despite the war hysteria the countless German-American clubs and associations had not been destroyed. In New York alone, there were more than two hundred, several of them like the New York *Turnverein* and the *Rheinischer Sänger-bund* now more than a century old. Gradually the leaders of the various groups took heart again. At the suggestion of Dr. Ludwig Oberndorf, the tireless editor of the *Staats-Zeitung,* delegates from all over the nation met in New York, in 1927 and organized the *Deutschamerikanischer National Kongress.* The formation of a central organization of a given ethnic group did not arouse any hostility at that time, for not only had the war hysteria subsided, but a new philosophy about minorities had grown up. The United States was no longer to be considered a huge melting pot in which foreign groups were melted down, losing their cultural traits and ethnic identity. America was now a beautiful mosaic composed of many variegated stones of different shapes and colors. It was a symphony orchestra in which there were many different types of instruments, all contributing to a splendid harmony. The term "Americanization" was no longer used.

German-Americans were proud of their vigorous support of the Victory Loan. The sincerity of this could not be doubted, for they, like everyone else in the country, had been involved in the war. Their sons had enlisted; many of them did not return. Also, it was a source of pride to read the letters of many American soldiers, who had found Germany so clean and orderly and of others who had married German girls.

As early as 1920, German Day celebrations were revived. The Steuben Society of America was founded to promote the interest of the group through political participation and action. In 1930, the Carl Schurz Memorial Foundation was organized to promote cultural relations between the United States and Germany.

The German language press, however, had taken an awful beating during the war. Because of the enforced censorship,

the hostility of superpatriots, and the government require-
ment of the translation of war articles, many had not been
able to weather the storm. In 1914, there were 537 German
language publications in the United States, including 53 daily
newspapers. In 1917, the number of publications had dropped
to 489; by 1920, there were only 278.

Nevertheless, things were looking up for the German-Americans when, again, ominous clouds appeared on the European
horizon. Increasingly large demonstrations were being held in
German cities, led by a fanatic rabble-rouser named Adolf
Hitler. At first, the obscure, humorless housepainter and ex-
sergeant was laughed at as a harmless mountebank. As his
following increased and his utterances became more and more
vicious, it was evident that there would be trouble. And what
trouble!

5. A SECOND BLOODBATH

Threatening events succeeded one another on the Continent
with startling rapidity. On Jan. 30, 1933, Hitler became
Chancellor; on Feb. 28, the *Reichstag* fire occurred; in 1935,
Hitler rejected the Versailles Treaty; and in 1936, he had his
soldiers occupy the demilitarized Rhineland.

As in the case of the First World War, most Americans had
no desire to enter the conflict. This was true of German-
Americans, too. Some of them in the beginning were filled
with admiration for Hitler, the strong man, the dauntless hero
who would raise Germany out of the slough of despondency.
When they saw the turn of events, however, they turned aside
in disgust.

In general, the Nazis had no regard for world opinion; they
relied on their might. They did, however, make crude and
brutal attempts to bludgeon German-Americans and drag
them into their camp. A vicious rowdy named Spanknöbel
tried to intimidate German-American businessmen and editors. When he entered the offices of the *Staats-Zeitung* one
morning to introduce his *Gleichschaltung,* he was almost
ejected bodily. His successor, Fritz Kuhn, did not fare much

better. Kuhn, however, did score certain successes. He formed a *Nazi Bund* and published his own paper, the *Deutscher Weckruf und Beobachter*. It never had a circulation of more than five thousand; usually it was distributed free.

The German language papers were highly embarrassed by the events in Germany and by Nazi propaganda. Some of the older papers like the *Staats-Zeitung* and the *Rochester Abend-post* tried to avoid the issue; others like the Socialist *Volks-zeitung* were violently anti-Nazi.

Many German-Americans deplored the illegal acts and the brutalities of the Nazis, but they missed one excellent opportunity. That was an unequivocal, straightforward denunciation of Hitler's anti-Jewish policy. This should not have been difficult, for many German Jews had worked wholeheartedly in German-American societies, and many had made distinct cultural contributions.

It is needless here to recount the course of the war. Again German-Americans, like their fellow countrymen, gave their money and the lives of their sons to win the battle. Naturally, it was heart-rending for them to read of the saturation bombing of the beautiful cities of the Fatherland. And as for the atrocities of Hitler's minions, they ignored them as mere war propaganda.

The plight of the Jews was unspeakable. They began leaving Germany soon after Hitler got into power. The largest number came to the United States in 1938. Many Christians, too, who had incurred the wrath of the Nazis, fled including the well-known writer Thomas Mann. In these years over a hundred thousand persons fled from Germany. Many of them, especially among the Jews, were cultured and professionally trained. Germany was the loser, America the gainer by this vast exodus. One of the greatest minds of all time came to the United States: Albert Einstein. He received a call from Princeton, where he worked in the Institute for Advanced Studies. Other distinguished German Jews formed the University in Exile which became the New School.

It is remarkable that, despite their terrible sufferings and the loss of their homes and relatives, they still felt themselves a part of the Germanic group. In New York they founded a German language newspaper, *Aufbau,* which in 1955 had a circulation of twenty-nine thousand. There were theater performances and lectures. The refugees greatly raised the cultural level of German America.

It is worth noting that during the Second World War the hysterical hatred of everything German did not manifest itself as it did during World War I. No attempt was made to suppress the German tongue. In fact, it was included in the propaganda pamphlets issued by the government. German enrollments in the schools did drop, but the language did not drop out entirely. In fact, in some cases there were increases, since the children of the refugees, who spoke German, were placed in advanced classes. The Army, too, realized the immense advantage of knowing the language of the enemy. The Army Specialized Training Program maintained German as one of its chief language courses.

The mistakes of the First World War were not repeated.

6. THE REFUGEES

The position of the Jews in Germany became increasingly precarious as the Nazis gained in power. Having survived countless outbursts of anti-Semitism and relying on the fact that their ancestors had been loyal members of the German community for more than five hundred years, many Jews did not think the situation was too serious. They relied on the sense of justice and decency of the German people. Since they thought the storm would soon blow over, they remained until the very last moment.

Others, however, saw which way the wind was blowing and decided to get away before the hurricane burst upon them. They sold their homes and businesses and left for other countries. From 1933 on, about 140,000 German Jews came to the United States. They came from all walks of life and all age groups. In 1953, about 20 per cent were over 65 years old.

Not only did Jewish organizations give them immediate help

on their arrival, but many Christian groups, like the Quakers, provided for them. Fortunately most of them were not urgently in need of assistance, for they were mainly of the middle and upper middle class, having brought along financial means and works of art. There were artisans, skilled workers, and clerks. On the whole, they were well-educated people with a ratio of professionals almost four times as high as that shown in the immigrant statistics for the previous decade.

Because of their professional experience and training, the cry soon arose that they were taking jobs away from native Americans. Actually, they were a labor-creating group. They opened up shops and factories; they introduced new products and new processes. In a sampling of 158 refugee-owned manufacturing concerns, it was found that 69 were producing goods not previously made in this country; 50 had introduced new products; and 22, new processes.

The refugees distinguished themselves from native American Jews in a number of ways. As cultured Europeans, accustomed to high standards of living, they were somewhat critical of American life. Many of them had not been strongly conscious of their Jewish background; in fact, they considered themselves Germans. On German records the terminology used was, *mosaischen Glaubens* ("of Mosaic belief"). They spoke neither Hebrew nor Yiddish; their language was the best High German.

Despite their unspeakably cruel treatment at the hands of the Nazis, they brought with them and continued to maintain the language and culture of their native land. German was their language of communication at home, in their clubs, and on the street. In New York one heard better German more frequently on Washington Heights, where many refugees had settled, than in Yorkville, the traditional German-American quarter. A number of refugees started German publishing houses, such as *Schocken Verlag, Frederick Ungar* and *Erga*. Well-known Jewish authors from Germany like Herman Broch, Lion Feuchtwanger, Emil Ludwig, and Franz Werfel continued to write in German.

157

The refugees contributed greatly to the material welfare of the communities in which they settled, but, more significantly, they raised the level of German culture in the United States far beyond anything attained previously except through the Forty-Eighters. The fury of Hitler gave Thomas Mann and Albert Einstein to America.

7. PEACE

The German language press, however, had sustained severe losses. In 1920, there were still 278 German publications in the United States. In 1930, there were 172, and by 1950, the total had dropped to a mere 60. Only a dozen German language newspapers were left in the entire country. Before World War I, New York alone had supported five German dailies. It should be pointed out that other foreign languages sustained similar losses. The Yiddish press in New York has declined perceptibly. Only in Spanish, through the great influx of Puerto Ricans and Cubans, has there been expansion.

The decline is due in great part to the diminishing numbers of immigrants. Whereas in 1905, 1906, and 1907 more than 1,000,000 persons a year entered the United States; from 1932 to 1945, the totals from all countries were less than 83,000 annually; in 1958, the figure was slightly over 250,000. The German quota—and it is hardly filled—is only 25,814.

Furthermore, the type of German who emigrates is quite different from his compatriot of former years. He has usually learned some English (English is taught in German schools from the fifth year on). He is not suffering from religious or political persecution; he is eager to get on. Hence, he does not care to be identified as a German; he wants to become an American as fast as possible. His advent means no gain for German-American societies or the German language press.

Through the remarkable energy of its people and through the boundless generosity of America and its Marshall Plan, Germany has recovered within an astoundingly short period. Because of its rapid economic recovery it is called the *Wirtschaftswunder*. Its currency is the strongest in Europe; its government is one of the most stable in the world. Largely through the tact and sagacity of its venerable Konrad Adenauer, the West German Republic has regained the respect of the world. It is one of America's most reliable allies. The German people have demonstrated that they can function under a democratic form of government. Relations with France, too, have become cordial. Germany is one of the strongest members of NATO. And brave Berlin has become the bulwark of Western democracy.

The close political and military relations between the United States and Germany have greatly raised the morale of German-Americans. In New York each fall a Steuben Parade is held on Fifth Avenue with beautiful historic floats. It is overt evidence of the strength of the German element in the largest American city. Its stress on the historic contributions of the Germans in the United States is a manifestation of their love for America and their desire to be considered an integral part of its texture.

Summary

From the preceding pages it is hoped that the reader has obtained a rather clear, factual, and sympathetic picture of the Germans in America. A few words of comment are in order at this point.

In the first place, it is evident that the Germans form the largest non-English group in the United States. They constitute a little more than one-fourth of the entire foreign element in the country. Although at first they were exceeded by the Irish numerically, the Germans overtook them by 1851. During the nineteenth century, 3,871,253 immigrants came from Ireland, and 5,009,280 from Germany. In addition, a large proportion of the 1,027,195 from Austria-Hungary spoke German. It has been estimated that at least one-fifth of all Americans have German blood in their veins.

Germans came over at various times for different reasons: religious persecution, political oppression, wretched economic conditions, and a desire to escape military service. They were attracted to the United States by the many enthusiastic reports and books which appeared in Europe, extolling the grandeur of the landscape and the freedom of the individual. Germans settled in every one of the Colonies; they are the most evenly distributed of any of the foreign ethnic groups.

The large majority of Germans, despite initial hardships and sufferings, became successful, prosperous, and devoted citizens of the United States. They helped to build the nation and made notable contributions in every field of human endeavor. Hundreds of thousands of them died on battlefields to secure independence, to preserve the Union, and to protect our democratic institutions. However, considering their numbers, the Germans were not as outstanding as some other ethnic groups in the field of politics. There were some outstanding figures, though, who helped to shape the policies of our government. In this field Carl Schurz was the most eminent German-American.

Although every level of society and every type of political point of view has been represented among them, these extremes quickly blended into the body of traditional Americanism. A classic example of this are the Forty-Eighters, some of whom were aristocrats, some of whom were peasants; some of whom were monarchists, some of whom were communists.

The Germans have always been sober, thrifty, and solid citizens. Despite their large numbers, they have contributed far below the average to vagrancy, delinquency, and crime. Even in Colonial times British governors were eager to secure them as settlers in the Colonies.

Bibliography

The Germans have produced a vast amount of material about the United States; they call it *Amerika-Literatur*. Faust provides an extensive bibliography which runs to eighty-two pages. Almost all of the titles are in German; a large portion of them are of interest only to the scholar and the specialist. In addition to Faust, we list below only a few of the more recent books in English which may be of interest to the general reader.

FAUST, ALBERT B.: *The German Element in the United States.* 2 volumes, New York, The Steuben Society of America, 1927.

HIRSHLER, ERIC E.: *Jews from Germany in the United States.* New York, Farrar, Straus & Cudahy, 1955.

SKAL, G. V.: *History of German Immigration in the United States.* New York, 1908.

SOCIETY FOR THE HISTORY OF THE GERMANS IN MARYLAND: *Twenty-eighth Report,* 1953. *Twenty-ninth Report,* 1956, Baltimore, Md.

WEBER, PAUL C.: *America in Imaginative German Literature.* New York, Columbia University Press, 1926.

WITTKE, CARL: *The German-Language Press in America.* Lexington, University of Kentucky Press, 1957.

——— *Refugees of Revolution: The German Forty-Eighters in America.* Philadelphia, 1952.

——— *We Who Built America: The Saga of the Immigrant.* New York, 1939.

ZUCKER, A. E.: *The Forty-Eighters*. New York, Columbia University Press, 1950.

*   *   *

The American German Review, published by the Carl Schurz Memorial Foundation in Philadelphia, presents articles on German-American life in each issue.

Index

167

168

DATE DUE